BRIDGEPORT
BASEBALL

To my father, Roman Bielawa, who told me about
Mohawk Mills Park and the 1940s Class C Amsterdam Rugmakers,
and to my grandfather, Joe Makarowski, who shared memories of eight-
hour Model T rides, flat tires, and full whiskey bottles that led to watch-
ing the Babe hit home runs. This book is dedicated to you both.

BRIDGEPORT
BASEBALL

Michael J. Bielawa

ARCADIA
PUBLISHING

Copyright © 2003 by Michael J. Bielawa
ISBN 978-1-5316-0798-2

Published by Arcadia Publishing
Charleston, South Carolina

Library of Congress Catalog Card Number: 2003103001

For all general information, contact Arcadia Publishing:
Telephone 843-853-2070
Fax 843-853-0044
E-mail sales@arcadiapublishing.com
For customer service and orders:
Toll-free 1-888-313-2665

Visit us on the Internet at www.arcadiapublishing.com

Unless otherwise noted, images throughout this book are courtesy of the Michael J. Bielawa collection.

On the cover: Background, the 1914 Bridgeport Bolts (photograph courtesy of Corbit Studios); front left, James O'Rourke (photograph courtesy of Historical Collections, Bridgeport Public Library); front right, Angel Espada of the 2002 Bluefish (photograph courtesy of Robert Levy Photography); back cover, the Ballpark at Harbor Yard on opening day in 1999 (photograph courtesy of Morgan Kaolian/AEROPIX).

CONTENTS

ACKNOWLEDGMENTS

This book was made possible by the many fans of Bridgeport baseball. I received assistance from individuals across North America and as far away as England and Japan. I wish to express appreciation to my boss, Michael Golrick (Bridgeport city librarian), for his support. Special thanks go to Mary Witkowski, head of Bridgeport Public Library Historical Collections, and her talented staff, Elizabeth Van Tuyl, Roseanne Mansfield, Benjamin Ortiz, Luis Rodriguez, Sarah Greenberg, and Jennifer Samath. Thanks are also due Gerald Sabo inter-library loan specialist extraordinaire. Acknowledgment is also due Bill Burdick, who makes wishes come true at the Baseball Hall of Fame in Cooperstown, New York, and to Mark Rucker and Transcendental Graphics. Thanks also to the Society for American Baseball Research (SABR), especially Martin Abramowitz, J.P. Caillant, Bill Gilbert, Bill Hickman, G. Reed Howard, Stephen Milman, Yoichi Nagata, Andy North, Gary Otake, Paul Reiferson, Eric Sallee, Paul Sallee, Steve Steinberg, David Stevens, Dennis VanLangen, and Tom Zeiler. Jewish Major Leaguers Inc. Bridgeport baseball is alive and well due to the owners of the Bridgeport Bluefish of the independent Atlantic League, Mickey Herbert, Ken Paul, Mary-Jane Foster, Jack McGregor, Ira Perkins, Bridgeport Waterfront Investors, and Charlie Dowd (co-owner and general manager). Very special thanks, a hot dog, and bottle of Moet go to Chris Romano, public and media relations manager. Chris, without you this book would have never happened. John Farrell, of many hats in the Bluefish front office, your humor and friendship are embraced by my family and me. The outstanding gentlemen of the Greater Bridgeport Oldtimer's Athletic Association, especially Mickey Buckmir and Charlie Rich, for loaning me photographs. Thanks to Ben Murphy for sharing baseball memories on a rainy afternoon. To the members and families of the Bridgeport Bears and Bees, warmhearted thanks for telling me about your wonderful experiences, especially Diane (Michaels) Prucinsky, Kitty (Michaels) and John Midney, Fritz Luciano, Vinny Noce and Sally and Duke Sherwood. Jim Paules, you are a baseball genius and a dear friend. The Bears and Bees live on in all of you! Bridgeport superstars Phil Nastu and Nick Giaquinto. Thanks to Paul Conan, the great-great-grandson of James O'Rourke, and Laurie, his wife. Paul, we'll always have right field covered at Newfield. Mary Lai, Buck Lai Sr.'s daughter-in-law, a lovely and thoughtful person. Bridgeport baseball experts Bernie Crowley and Frank Williams, your wisdom is inspiring. Frank is an authority on Bridgeport minor-league statistics and James O'Rourke minor-league statistics. Fred and Violet Biebel, Len Benedetto Jr., Bob Levy, Craig Kelly, Rob Medina, and the Chicago Historical Society; Aaron Schmidt at Boston Public Library; photographer Frank Decerbo Jr.; Janet Marks; the folks at the Stratford, Connecticut town hall: town planner Dave Killeen; Department of Engineering: Kevin Morrissey, Michael Hutman, and town engineer John Casey, secretary to town manager Helen Sadowski; and network administrator Erin McGuire-Kelley, Thomas Connor of the Bridgeport Firefighters Historical Society, Harry Hleva and the staff of the Igor I. Sikorsky Historical Archives Inc., Bridgeport City Hall's Engineering Department, Charles Brilvitch, Bob Harrison, Morgan Kaolian, David Davidowski, and Steve Raguskus. Three cheers to Janet Fisher and Nancy Sweeney for reading microfilm and proofing the chapters. Photographer Ed Brinsko and family. A special thank-you to all the unknown photographers whose works over the years preserved baseball history. I want to express gratitude to my editor, Tiffany Howe, whose guidance brought these pages to life. A special hug goes to a beautiful baseball fan who happens to be my wife, Janice. Thanks for letting me clutter our home with notes, books, and a few late-night shouts. This book is wholly possible because of your love. Finally, thanks to the people of Bridgeport who shared their baseball memories. To all of you here listed, and many others space does not allow me to name, this is your family photo album. Now, play ball!

INTRODUCTION

Bridgeport is baseball. The game has ruled after-work and out-of-school hours for 100 Connecticut summers. The legacy of the city's professional teams ushering local heroes to the majors, Senior City's century-old league, Industrial, Mercantile, Holy Name, Junior City, and Police Leagues, among others, all played (and still play) a vibrant role in the Park City's history.

The game provided an afternoon escape from 19th-century factory drudgery. Today, it offers an evening out with the family. The game embraces a continuity of sweet Junes and generations of fathers and mothers and sons and daughters wearing Bridgeport baseball uniforms. Barnstorming African American teams, Major League exhibition contests sporting future Hall of Famers, and the bond shared between fans and players are all a part of Bridgeport's landscape. Base paths have always been a right of passage for children, of course, but for immigrants, too. Baseball helped citizens become American and helped America become a greater nation.

Baseball is underfoot everywhere in Bridgeport. It was a challenge when creating this book to decide which images represented a particular player, team, or era. When discussing a player seasoned on Bridgeport diamonds, it was necessary in some cases to use a photograph from their Major League days. Since the business of baseball takes place both on and off the field, photographs depicting Bridgeport's important baseball places are also featured. The goal was always to present the overall story of Bridgeport baseball. It is hoped that this book will cause readers to reminisce, to learn, and to do what baseball lovers do best—to "talk baseball." This book is more than a history. It is a living family album. The family includes every player and fan whose heart has ever been touched by this city ruled by baseball.

One

THE LIFE OF ORATOR JIM, BRIDGEPORT'S HALL OF FAMER

THE OSCEOLA BASE BALL CLUB, C. 1870. James Henry O'Rourke was born in East Bridgeport on September 1, 1850. In 1870, the future Hall of Famer was catching and playing infield with the local Osceolas. The name Osceola was inspired by the 1830s Seminole Indian leader. Commenting about the game as it was played in the 1870s, O'Rourke explained, "There was no paraphernalia with which one could protect himself. No mitts; no, not even gloves; and masks, why you would have been laughed off the diamond had you worn one behind the bat." (Photograph courtesy of Corbit Studios.)

BOSTON Base Ball Club.

PLAYERS.	Pos.	1	2	3	4	5	6	7	8	9	O.	R.	B.
1. G. Wright,	SS												
2. Barnes,	2d												
3. Leonard,	LF												
4. McVey,	C												
5. Spaulding,	P												
6. Gould,	1st												
7. Schafer,	3d												
8. Rogers,	RF												
9. H. Wright,	CF												
Totals.													

Scorer, Umpire,

MANSFIELD Base Ball Club.

PLAYERS.	Pos.	1	2	3	4	5	6	7	8	9	O.	R.	B.
1. Clapp,	C												
2. Buttey,	RF												
3. Bentley,	P												
4. Muman,	1st												
5. Booth,	2d												
6. Tipper,	3d												
7. O'Rourke,	SS												
8. McCarton,	CF												
9. Fields,	LF												
Totals.													

Scorer, Time of Game, Hrs. Min.

PRINTING of every description executed with Neatness and Dispatch, at THE RICE, GODDARD & CO., Printing Establishment, No. 41 Milk Street, Boston.

O'ROURKE'S FIRST MAJOR-LEAGUE SEASON SCORECARD. Connecticut's first major-league team was the Middletown Mansfields, named after Gen. Joseph Mansfield. Manager Ben Douglas signed O'Rourke in April 1872. According to legend, O'Rourke would not leave his widowed mother, Catherine, until Douglas promised to hire a hand to help on the family farm. O'Rourke played with Middletown during their sole season in the National Association. Financial difficulties compelled the team to disband in August 1872. (Scorecard courtesy of Transcendental Graphics.)

THE 1874 NATIONAL ASSOCIATION BOSTON RED STOCKINGS. Manager Harry Wright signed O'Rourke as an infielder in 1873. When the National League was born in 1876, the team became known as the Boston Red Caps. Jim O'Rourke is credited with getting the first hit in National League history, a two out single to left in the top of the first inning on opening day, April 22, 1876, against Philadelphia. In this photograph, O'Rourke is seated on the far left. (Photograph courtesy of Historical Collections, Bridgeport Public Library.)

THE 1874 TOUR. The Boston Red Stockings and Philadelphia Athletic Club toured England and Ireland touting baseball in 1874. From July 30 to late August, the 22 Americans played local cricket teams, and Boston and Philadelphia played baseball against one another. Spectators were sorely puzzled at first, but "brilliant fielding and catching of both sides in the first innings soon produced an outburst of applause." (Illustration courtesy of Transcendental Graphics.)

JUMP TO PROVIDENCE. In 1879, O'Rourke objected to the team's practice of deducting $20 per season to pay for uniforms. As a result, he left the Red Caps along with teammate George Wright. This decision would have far-reaching implications for baseball for nearly a century. Reeling over their departure, Boston owner Arthur Soden instituted the reserve clause, which, in effect, bound players to a team for life. Meanwhile, Jim and George (as manager) helped their new team, the Providence Grays, capture the 1879 Championship. The Boston Red Caps (left) and Providence Grays (right) line up for a photograph at Providence's Messer Park in 1879. O'Rourke is standing third from the left with his Grays teammates. (Photograph courtesy of National Baseball Hall of Fame Library, Cooperstown, New York.)

THE FIRST BROTHERS TO PLAY THE SAME MAJOR LEAGUE OUTFIELD. When James O'Rourke left for Providence, his brother John (1849–1911) was signed with Boston. John is pictured here in 1879, the year he batted .341. When James returned to the Red Caps in 1880, they became the first Major League brothers to patrol the outfield together. In 1883, John was playing for the American Association New York Metropolitans (the original Mets) and was known for his headfirst slides. One such attempt resulted in an injury that ended his career. (Photograph courtesy of National Baseball Hall of Fame Library, Cooperstown, New York.)

BUFFALO BOUND. James O'Rourke played one last season in Boston before signing with the Buffalo Bisons as player-manager from 1881 to 1884. Other future Hall of Famers on this club included Pud Galvin and Dan Brouthers. Jim had rediscovered Big Dan, the former first sacker for the Troy Trojans, digging sewer ditches and easily convinced him to drop the shovel and pick up a bat in Buffalo. (Photograph courtesy of Paul Conan genealogy collection.)

BATTING PROWESS, 1884. O'Rourke's final season with Buffalo was one of his best. He finished in the top two in the league in four offensive categories: batting (first place with .347), hits (tied for first with 162), runs scored (second with 119), and doubles (second with 33). Just as in 1881, O'Rourke managed the Bisons to third place, their highest showing while Jim was at the helm. (Illustration from *Spalding's Official Base Ball Guide*, 1885.)

JAMES THE GIANT. During the 1884 campaign, New York made an offer to Jim to leave Buffalo. The contract would have made him the highest paid player in the game. Known for his integrity as well as his hitting, Jim refused the offer and waited until the start of the next season to join the New York Giants for their 1885 inaugural season. This was the first year New York's National League club was known as the Giants. During their first two years of existence (1883–1884), they were called the Gothams. (Photograph courtesy of Historical Collections, Bridgeport Public Library.)

THE ORATOR. Tapped for a loan by a teammate, the Orator instantly replied, "The exigencies of the occasion and the condition of the exchequer will not permit anything of the sort." Rounding the bases after delivering what he thought was a homer, but informed by the umpire that the ball was foul, Jim launched this verbal assault: "I am conversant with the conglomeration of facts in this case, and as my optical eyesight is of extreme excellence, I am positive of your misinformation." (Photograph courtesy of Transcendental Graphics.)

ORATOR JIM ATTENDS YALE LAW. Already regarded for his propensity to pummel opponents, umpires, and teammates with grandiloquent tongue-lashings, O'Rourke pursued another career where his flair for verbiage would be welcome. Orator Jim convinced the Giants to pay his tuition and attended Yale Law School during the off-season. He graduated in 1887. Edith Hanke, James O'Rourke's youngest daughter, reminisced with baseball historian Lee Allen in 1968 that her father always scolded her with five-syllable words. (Illustration from *Harper's Weekly*, May 16, 1885.)

O'ROURKE IN NEW YORK. James
began playing for the National League
New York Giants in 1885, when their
stadium really was a polo grounds,
located at the northern
edge of Central Park between
Fifth and Sixth Avenues from 110th
to 112th Streets. The Giants were
evicted from the Polo Grounds
in 1889. (Illustration courtesy of
Transcendental Graphics.)

JIM O'ROURKE, 3d B. N. Y's.

GOODWIN & CO. New York.

SYMPATHETIC TO PLAYERS' RIGHTS. O'Rourke jumped
to the New York Players League entry, also called the
Giants, in 1890. (This photograph is dated 1887.)
Games were played in Brotherhood Park adjacent to
the National League Giants' new stadium, Manhattan
Field, better known as the New Polo Grounds (Polo
Grounds II), below Coogan's Bluff. After the Players
League collapsed at the end of 1890 (Jim batted .360),
the National League Giants moved into Brotherhood
Park and changed the name to the Polo Grounds (Polo
Grounds III). O'Rourke returned to the National
League Giants for 1891–1892.

15

ARBITER O'ROURKE. Orator Jim became the player-manager for the Washington Senators in 1893, his final full season in the National League. A short stint at umpiring followed in 1894, but the occupation ran against the Orator's kindheartedness. The June 29, 1894 *Bridgeport Evening Post* consoled, "Abuse by the press and the bleachers has driven Jim O'Rourke from his position as umpire. He was a thoroughly conscientious umpire, but he did not have the hide of a rhinoceros over his sensitivities."

ORATOR JIM RETURNS TO BRIDGEPORT. The remaining summer months of 1894 saw O'Rourke play for a number of city teams (including the St. Josephs, YMCA, and the East Side Athletics). Securing the best local talent, he formed the Bridgeport Victors in May 1895. One month later, he helped establish the Connecticut State League. The Victors won the championship in an abbreviated season, and in 1896, the league changed its name to the Naugatuck Valley League. Again, the Victors captured the pennant. The 1896 Naugatuck Valley League champions are, from left to right, as follows: (first row) Terrance Rogers, Patrick Cunningham, James O'Rourke, C. Howard Dunbar, and Jack Doherty; (back row) Jack Kelly, Jack Dempsey, Philip Blansfield, Clarence "Pop" Foster, Harry Herbert, and Richard Mansfield. (Photograph courtesy of Historical Collections, Bridgeport Public Library.)

NEWFIELD PARK, 1898. The O'Rourke brothers owned land in Bridgeport's Newfield neighborhood. Jim converted their family's old farm into a ballpark, and the first game played at Newfield Grounds pitted O'Rourke's newly named Orators in an exhibition contest against Springfield of the Eastern League on Friday the 13th of May 1898. The first of a long lineup of future Hall of Famers to play here was not Orator Jim. That day, his friend Big Dan Brouthers played first base for the visiting team. (Photograph courtesy of Transcendental Graphics.)

POLITICO BEHIND THE PLATE. Catcher-attorney O'Rourke was dedicated to Bridgeport, and he served as city fire commissioner and as a member of the paving and sewer commission. O'Rourke's run-ins with Mayor Denis Mulvihill were legendary. It was reported that police were often summoned to city hall to interrupt their spirited debates. Jim was also a member of the Bridgeport municipal baseball team, pictured here in 1902. Jim is standing seventh from left. City clerk and future mayor E.T. Buckingham is seated on the far left. The austere-looking fellow wearing the dark suit is Mayor Mulvihill. (Photograph courtesy of Historical Collections, Bridgeport Public Library.)

THE FIRST TO PLAY MAJOR-LEAGUE BALL IN FOUR DIFFERENT DECADES. Deep down, John McGraw, the fiery New York Giants manager must have had a soft heart. He invited Orator Jim back to the Polo Grounds to play one more game. On September 22, 1904, 54-year-old James O'Rourke caught a complete game thrown by "Iron Man" Joe McGinnity, making Jim the first person to play major-league ball in four different decades. During the game, Jim singled to center in four at bats and scored a run. (Photograph courtesy of National Baseball Hall of Fame Library, Cooperstown, New York.)

THE ORATOR AND QUEENIE, FATHER AND SON TEAMMATES. Orator Jim (left) and his son James Stephen "Queenie" O'Rourke (1883–1955) were teammates on the Orators from 1903 to 1908. In his final year with the Orators, Queenie was signed by the New York Highlanders and played 34 games with the American League squad. This club would soon be known as the New York Yankees. Afterward, Queenie played in the American Association with the Columbus Senators and St. Paul Saints. He retired from professional ball in 1914.

NEW HAVEN BASE BALL CLUB. CONN. LEAGE 1912

ORATOR JIM'S LAST PROFESSIONAL GAME. Forty years after O'Rourke first stepped onto a Major League diamond, he enjoyed one final professional game with the Connecticut League champion New Haven White Wings. On September 14, 1912, fans witnessed the 62-year-old league president catch a complete nine-inning contest against the last-place Waterbury Spuds. The game was played at Savin Rock in New Haven. The White Wings included Pop Foster, the ever-popular former outfielder with the Bridgeport Orators, and Dutch Sherwood, the father of future Bridgeport Bees co-owner and center fielder Bobby Sherwood.

ONE GAME A YEAR. Long after his days as a regular player with Bridgeport, O'Rourke faithfully appeared in one game each year with his beloved Elks Lodge No. 36. This *c.* 1916 photograph is one of the very last times Orator Jim donned a uniform. Frigid weather gripped Bridgeport the first few days of 1919. Despite the cold weather, attorney O'Rourke set out on foot to meet a client. Jim caught a cold that developed into pneumonia. After a four-day illness, on January 8, 1919, Orator Jim passed away. The funeral was held at the O'Rourke house (274 Pembroke Street), and his friend and fellow Hall of Famer Roger Connor was a pallbearer. James O'Rourke is buried in the family plot at St. Michael's cemetery. (Photograph courtesy of Paul Conan genealogy collection.)

O'ROURKE'S FAN CLUB, C. 1907.
Wherever the female members of
James O'Rourke's family gathered, they
formed their own rooting section. This
photograph shows, from left to right,
daughters Irene, Sadie, Lillian, Edith,
and Ida; wife Annie; and daughter
Agnes. (Photograph courtesy of Paul
Conan genealogy collection.)

THE JAMES O'ROURKE HOME. Constructed during 1891, the house was originally a single-family residence large enough to accommodate Jim's growing clan. At the beginning of the 21st century, the city acquired all adjacent property and razed the neighborhood to make this area business ready. The home now stands alone. It is hoped that it will be preserved as a museum to the Hall of Famer's memory, Irish-American heritage, and baseball history.

JAMES H. O'ROURKE

"ORATOR JIM" PLAYED BALL UNTIL HE
WAS PAST FIFTY, INCLUDING TWENTY-ONE
MAJOR LEAGUE SEASONS. AN OUTFIELDER
AND CATCHER FOR THE BOSTON RED
STOCKINGS OF 1873, HE LATER WORE
THE UNIFORMS OF THE CHAMPIONSHIP
PROVIDENCE TEAM OF 1879, BUFFALO,
NEW YORK AND WASHINGTON.

THE LEGACY OF BRIDGEPORT'S HALL OF FAMER. Orator Jim holds a special place in the history of the national game. He batted .300 or better 15 times and was a member of championship clubs in Boston, Providence, and New York. O'Rourke served as president of the Connecticut League and Eastern Association. Recognition for his contributions to baseball led to his enshrinement in the Hall of Fame in 1945. The legacy of Orator Jim still speaks volumes. Just read his plaque at Cooperstown. (Photograph courtesy of National Baseball Hall of Fame Library, Cooperstown, New York.)

Two

BASEBALL PLACES

SEASIDE AND BASEBALL. Baseball has been played on diamonds at Seaside Park dating back to the close of the Civil War. The most famous is Diamond No. 1, host to some of Bridgeport's earliest games as well as memorable Senior City and Industrial League contests. This photograph shows workers playing at Seaside *c.* 1915. The large American flag could indicate a Fourth of July or Labor Day ball game.

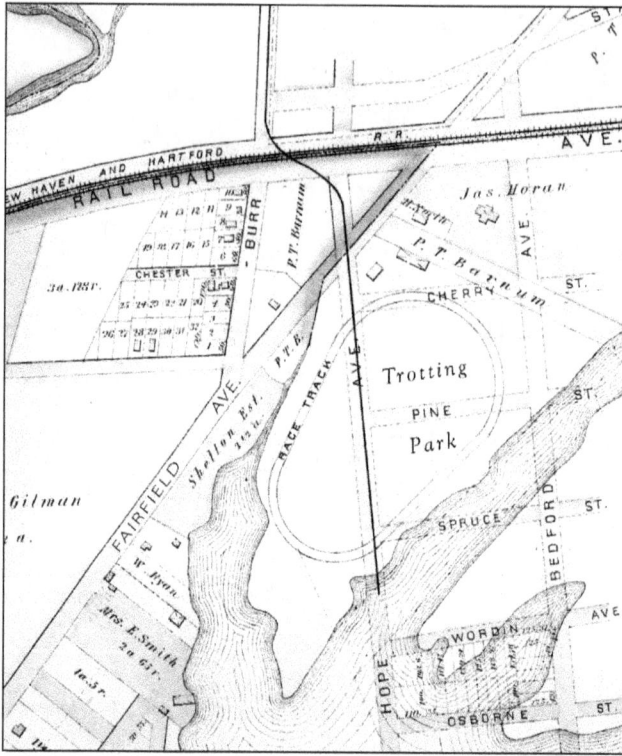

BASEBALL ON TRACK. Nineteenth-century ball games took place at the Bridgeport Trotting Park, located on Fairfield Avenue near the railroad tracks. Richard Sherwood, who leased the property to horse trainer William Cameron during the early 1870s, owned the park. In 1871, the Osceolas played the Middletown Mansfields here in one of their best-of-three series for the state championship. A group of former Osceolas reorganized the following summer as the Bridgeport Nine and played at Sherwood's Trotting Park. (Map from *Atlas of the City and Town of Bridgeport, Conn.* G.M. Hopkins, Philadelphia, 1888.)

THE BARNUM BALL GROUNDS. The city's first recognized professional team, the 1885 Bridgeport Giants of the Southern New England League, played their home games at the Barnum Ball Grounds. The park was located on the corner of State and Norman Streets (upper right-hand corner). In July 1885, neighbor N.S. Worden posted No Trespassing signs on his property to keep fans from climbing trees to watch games for free. Barnum housed his winter circus headquarters in the lower section of the park. (Map from *Atlas of the City and Town of Bridgeport, Conn.* G.M. Hopkins, Philadelphia, 1888.)

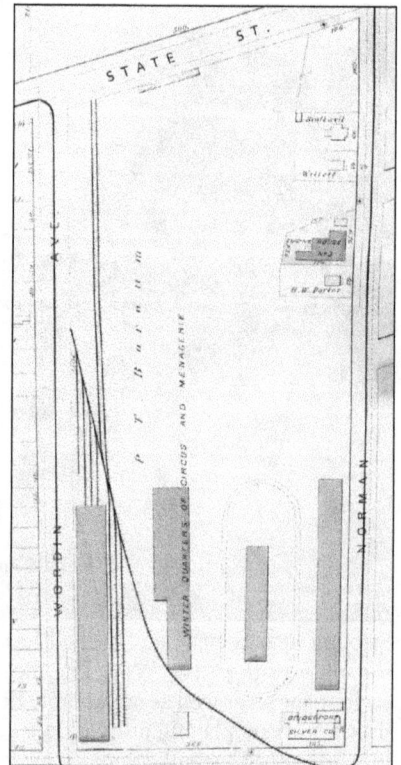

THE SILENT FAN. Built in 1885, Bridgeport Fire Department Engine House No. 3, on Norman Street, stood adjacent to the Barnum Ball Grounds. Fans likely filled the tower for a free view of games. When Buffalo Bill's Wild West Show visited the ball grounds in the summer of 1885, spectators crowded into the tower and were "glared" at throughout the show by performers. The bell was removed in September 1916, but the building remains to this day. (Photograph courtesy of Bridgeport Firefighters Historical Society.)

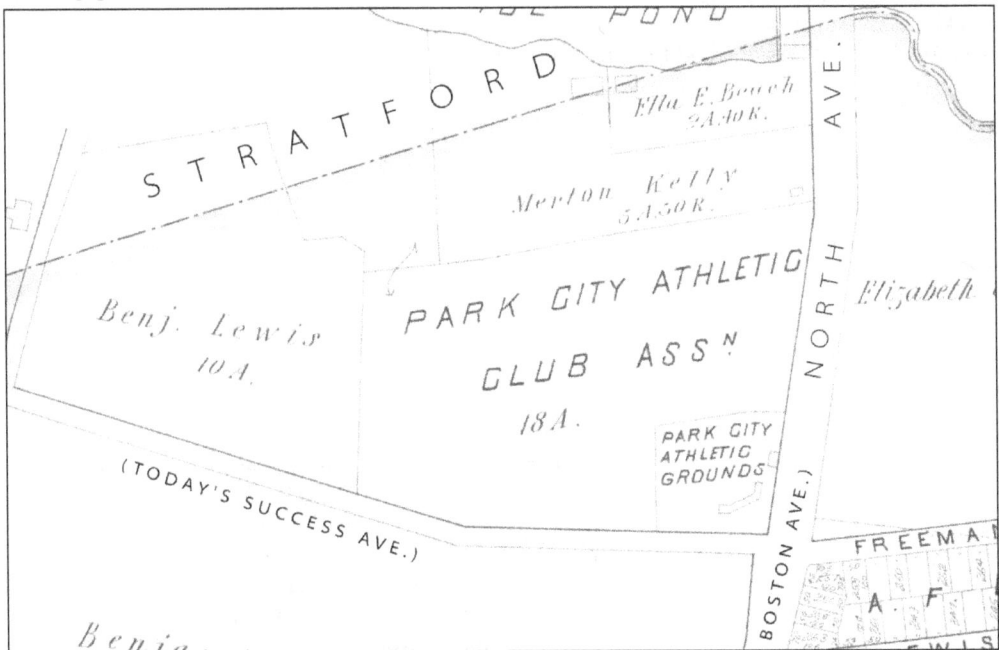

ATHLETIC PARK. Opening day in 1886 brought regular season contests to Athletic Park. The field was situated at the corner of Boston Avenue (then called North Avenue) and today's Success Avenue. To ensure a winning season that April, the Bridgeport Giants buried a horseshoe beneath home plate. (Map from *Atlas of the City of Bridgeport Connecticut*, D.L. Miller & Company, Philadelphia, 1896.)

Atlantic Hotel, Bridgeport, Conn.

THE ATLANTIC HOTEL. Located on the corner of Water Street and Fairfield Avenue across from the old railroad station, the Atlantic Hotel was home to visiting teams as far back as 1885. Bridgeport's hotels have always been a place for league administrators, management, players, reporters, and fans to congregate for the latest baseball gossip. The 1886 Bridgeport Giants stockholders and Eastern League owners held their meetings at the Atlantic. For decades, opening day parades kicked off from the front door of the Atlantic Hotel.

PLEASURE BEACH, 1896. A barrier island off the coast of Bridgeport, Pleasure Beach was opened as a private park in 1892. Two years later, a bicycle track and grandstand with seating for 2,000 were constructed. Bleachers on each side of the grandstand could accommodate an additional 3,000 fans. James O'Rourke, who returned to the city in 1894, eyed the new coliseum as a baseball stadium. Professional teams under James O'Rourke played there from 1895 to 1897. (Map from *Atlas of the City of Bridgeport Connecticut*, D.L. Miller & Company, Philadelphia, 1896.)

SURF AND BASEBALL TURF. The cover of this 1897 program illustrates three of the many attractions the island park offered—bicycle races, pristine beaches, and professional baseball. The Bridgeport Soubrettes divided home games between Pleasure Beach and Avon Park. Avon Park was located in West Stratford near the junction of Stratford and South Avenues. A baseball field was added in 1895. (Photograph courtesy of Historical Collections, Bridgeport Public Library.)

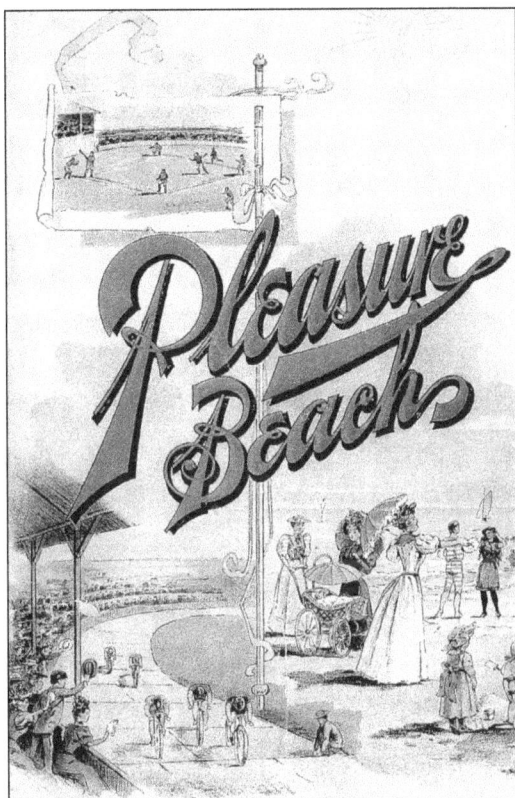

May	4	Bristol at Bridgeport.	July	10	Meriden at Bridgeport.
"	7	Torrington at Bridgeport.	"	14	Bristol at Bridgeport.
"	13	Derby at Bridgeport.	"	21	Derby at Bridgeport.
"	15	Waterbury at Bridgeport.	"	23	Waterbury at Bridgeport.
"	18	Meriden at Bridgeport.	"	29	Meriden at Bridgeport.
"	21	Torrington at Bridgeport.	"	31	Torrington at Bridgeport.
"	29	Waterbury at Bridgeport.	Aug.	3	Bristol at Bridgeport
"	31	Derby at Bridgeport (a.m.).	"	7	Torrington at Bridgeport.
June	5	Meriden at Bridgeport.	"	10	Derby at Bridgeport.
"	8	Torrington at Bridgeport.	"	13	Meriden at Bridgeport.
"	11	Bristol at Bridgeport.	"	17	Bristol at Bridgeport.
"	16	Waterbury at Bridgeport.	"	19	Torrington at Bridgeport.
"	18	Derby at Bridgeport.	"	26	Waterbury at Bridgeport.
"	23	Waterbury at Bridgeport.	"	31	Torrington at Bridgeport.
"	26	Meriden at Bridgeport.	Sept.	3	Meriden at Bridgeport.
"	30	Meriden at Bridgeport.	"	6	Derby at Bridgeport (a.m.).
July	1	Waterbury at Bridgeport.	"	11	Torrington at Bridgeport.
"	3	Bristol at Bridgeport.	"	14	Waterbury at Bridgeport.
"	5	Derby at Bridgeport (a. m.).			

THE OFFICIAL 1897 PLEASURE BEACH BASEBALL SCHEDULE. Fans were finding the 25¢ ferry ride, coupled with another 10¢ for a grandstand seat, too rich for their wallets. After the ferry ride, fans also had to walk a half-mile to and from the ball grounds. These disadvantages and the logistics of scheduling games between Pleasure Beach and Avon Park compelled O'Rourke to build a single, convenient ballpark—Newfield Grounds. (Photograph courtesy of Historical Collections, Bridgeport Public Library.)

SEA BREEZE ISLAND

THE IDEAL AMUSEMENT RESORT

Today: HARTFORD vs. BRIDGEPORT

Band Concerts, Bathing by Day or Moonlight, Roller Skating, Roller Coasting, Merry-Go-Round, Crazy House, Ferris Wheel, Tunnels of Love, Dancing, Cabaret Entertainments, Etc.

Seaview Avenue Cars run every minute via Golden Hill street loop after 2 o'clock. Boats run every few minutse from Stratford Avenue and Henry Street piers

A SEA BREEZE ISLAND ADVERTISEMENT. Pleasure Beach later became known as Steeplechase Island and Sea Breeze Island. After O'Rourke sold the Orators, regularly scheduled games were again played at the offshore diamond. In 1911, Bridgeport manager Gene McCann was arrested for playing a baseball game on Sunday here. This advertisement announces an August 11, 1912 Connecticut League baseball game as well as other attractions found at the resort. (Photograph courtesy of Historical Collections, Bridgeport Public Library.)

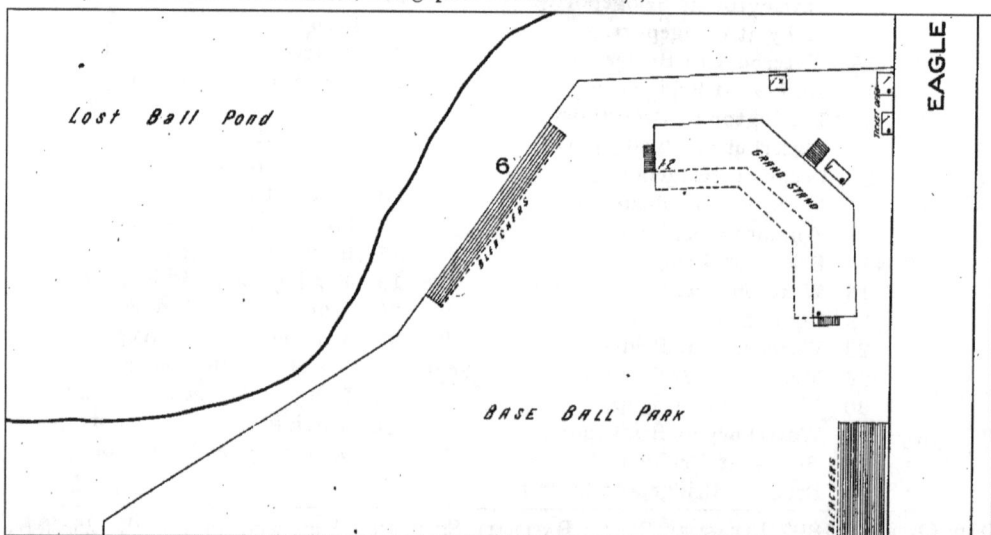

THE HISTORIC NEWFIELD GROUNDS, 1898–1932 AND 1941. Fans at Orator Jim's ball ground witnessed the first-ever regular season Connecticut League pitch, tossed at 3:30 p.m. on Wednesday, May 18, 1898. The swampy pond adjacent to Newfield's right-field boundary was poetically dubbed Lost Ball Pond. The deep left-field corner was located at the intersection of Eagle Street and Newfield Avenue, the site of today's backstop and home plate.

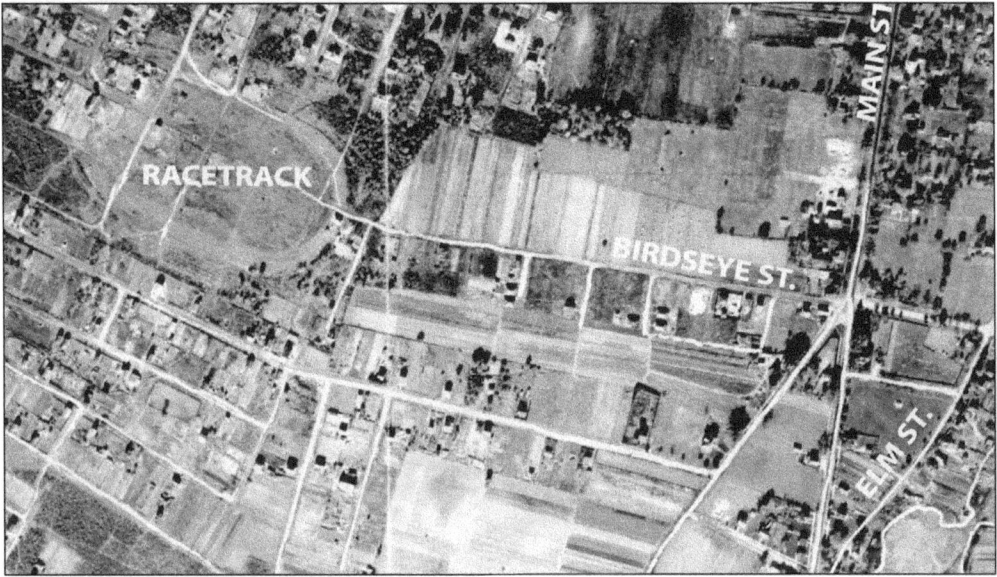

THE ORIGIN OF NEWFIELD'S GRANDSTAND. According to local legend, during Newfield Park's construction in 1898, James O'Rourke disassembled the old grandstand of the Stratford horse-racing track and moved it to his new park. The outline of the abandoned Stratford track was still visible in the late 1920s. Today, Johnson Academy rests in the approximate center of the oval along Birdseye Street. (Photograph courtesy of Stratford Town Hall, Department of Engineering, Stratford, Connecticut.)

NEWFIELD PARK DURING WORLD WAR I. The U.S. government issued its work-or-fight decree in May 1918, ordering all able-bodied men between the ages of 21 and 30 to find employment in essential war-related work by July 1918 or face military conscription. The Eastern League shut down on July 22, 1918, and Bridgeport ended its season in second place. Throughout the war, ballparks across America were the scene of patriotic rallies such as this one at Newfield. (Photograph courtesy of Historical Collections, Bridgeport Public Library.)

SEASIDE DIAMONDS NO. 1 AND NO. 5. Seaside's fabled Diamond No. 1, the site of many important Bridgeport baseball games, is shown here in 1919. It is the closer of the two ball fields in the upper right of this Brewer H. Sholund photograph, and Diamond No. 5 is in the background. The Perry Arch, at the bottom of Park Avenue, is seen on the left. (Photograph courtesy of Historical Collections, Bridgeport Public Library.)

THE STRATFIELD. This hotel opened in 1908 and became Bridgeport's baseball headquarters after World War I. Standing eight stories tall, it was the largest and best-equipped hotel between New York and Boston. On July 20, 1928, Merchant's Booster Day festivities kicked off with a unique and dangerous stunt. At 1:55 p.m., Bridgeport's Cuban first baseman Jose Rodriquez circled the pavement outside the Stratfield, waiting for Bears manager Billy Whitman to toss a baseball from the hotel's roof. Rodriquez made the catch.

DIAMONDS OF THE ROARING TWENTIES. This wonderful aerial shot was taken in October 1928. Newfield Park (left), home of the Bridgeport Bears, stands out among the homes of the city's East Side. Note the pitcher's alley between home plate and the mound. Leaving the neighborhood and following the lone road that crosses the Stratford marshes, you encounter the enclosed ball field known as Lordship Meadows (right). Once located on today's Lordship Boulevard, this was the home field of the Howards Athletic Club, one of Bridgeport's best African American baseball teams. (Photograph courtesy of Stratford Town Hall, Department of Engineering, Stratford, Connecticut.)

Night Baseball Lures Fan Bugs

NEW MOON OVER NEWFIELD, BRIDGEPORT'S FIRST NIGHT GAME. On the night of August 4, 1930, Mayor Buckingham flipped a switch, and Bridgeport baseball was forever changed. More than 6,000 fans had come out to see the Springfield Ponies play the Bridgeport Bears under the newly installed lights at Newfield. Two nights later, the New York Giants played an exhibition game under the lights and attracted Newfield's largest crowd—8,314.

NEWFIELD PARK, C. 1940. Newfield Park's last professional summer came in 1941, when the Inter-State League Bees moved here from York, Pennsylvania. Ironically, they were a farm club of the Boston Bees, the same club that was once known as the Red Caps, where Orator Jim O'Rourke got his National League start. The Bridgeport Bees finished the 1941 campaign second from last. Low attendance and America's entry into World War II doomed the team's return. (Photograph courtesy of U.S. Army Corps of Engineers, New England District.)

32

NEWFIELD'S SLOW DEMISE. After July 1932, Newfield Park became home to semiprofessional amateur and barnstorming baseball. In 1934, the field was used for a horse show (seen here). A track was installed, and midget auto races became a regular feature. After the Inter-State League Bridgeport Bees' single season in 1941, the old ballpark fell into disrepair. By April 1944, age and vandalism had taken their toll. Nonpayment of taxes led the city to foreclose and take title of Newfield. (Photograph courtesy of Historical Collections, Bridgeport Public Library.)

THE USUAL AUTUMN SCENE. Outside the Post Building on Cannon Street, the public could observe the progression of the 1916 World Series free of charge. The play board faced west to spare fans from having to look into the sun. Men perched on a narrow walkway at the base of the board changed lineups, moved runners around the bases, and posted balls, strikes, hits, and errors.

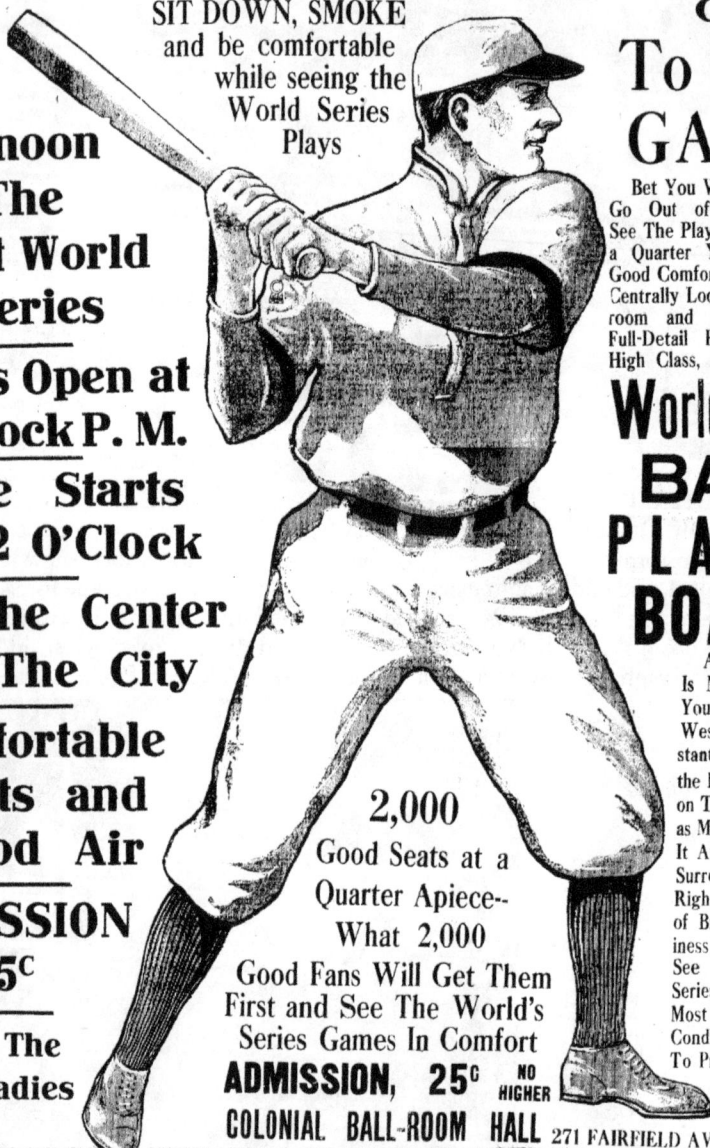

BASEBALL BEFORE TELEVISION. In the days before electronic media brought the World Series into homes at the flick of a switch, fans would assemble outside newspaper offices, in saloons, or in public halls to "watch" games. Lineups were posted, and as each play was telegraphed from faraway stadiums, staff would move figures around the diamond on a large board. This 1916 Colonial Ballroom advertisement from the *Bridgeport Telegram* invited men and women to enjoy the Fall Classic for only 25¢.

WHEN EVERY MAN WORE A HAT. The crowd here has gathered to "see" a game outside the Bridgeport Times-Star Building (formerly the Seaside Club, built in 1891), on the corner of Lafayette and State Streets. The date is Thursday, October 4, and the occasion is game one of the 1928 World Series. The New York Yankees, who won the opener 4-1, took the series from the St. Louis Cardinals in four games.

CANDIDATES FOR

DEATH

Each of these Automobile Daredevils FACE
DEATH every time they roll an automobile
end over end, jump a stock automobile
over a huge bus, crash two cars in a head
on collision or any of the 22 Great Thrillers
that will be seen in this Great Show!

Ward Beam's
WORLD'S CHAMPION AUTO DARE DEVILS

• ONE NITE ONLY •

FRIDAY JULY 16th, 8:30 P.M.

CANDLELITE STADIUM
RAIN DATE—JULY 17th

General Admission $1.25 — Kids 60c

RESERVED SEATS ON SALE AT CANDLELITE STADIUM

WHAT TO WATCH BEFORE REALITY TELEVISION, 1947–1950. Candlelite Stadium featured non-baseball attractions just as Newfield Park did. Candlelite Speedway's midget racecar track ran along the stadium's perimeter. Softball, boxing, and daredevil auto stunts, such as this one advertised in the 1948 *Bridgeport Telegram*, were a staple at the River Street facility.

SCHWARZ FIELD BECOMES CANDLELITE STADIUM, 1947. With the birth of the Class B Colonial League, Bridgeport's team owners, Carl Brunetto and Bobby Sherwood, acquired and converted River Street's Schwarz Field into a sports complex. Carl Brunetto is shown pointing at the old grandstand from the overgrown Schwarz infield. (Photograph courtesy of Duke Sherwood and family.)

THE BULLDOZED INFIELD. This aerial photograph shows the construction of Candlelite Stadium. Schwarz Field's grandstand was incorporated into the new stadium. (Photograph courtesy of Duke Sherwood and family.)

RACING THE CLOCK AT CANDLELITE. In the days before ballparks were built with concrete, steel, and plastic, the covered wooden bleachers along the left-field line were hammered into place. Note the huge puddles. Inclement weather caused endless construction delays and incredible deadlines. The first home game was finally played nine days late on Friday, May 16, 1947, against Poughkeepsie. This photograph was taken just 12 days earlier. (Photograph courtesy of Duke Sherwood and family.)

A STADIUM TAKES FORM. This May 1947 aerial shot shows the right-field bleachers going up. Candlelite Speedway's racetrack is easily visible, and Brunetto's Candlelite Restaurant, with the long front awning, is located beyond right field's short porch. Schwarz Brothers Lumberyard is seen in the lower right of the photograph, facing River Street. (Photograph courtesy of Duke Sherwood and family.)

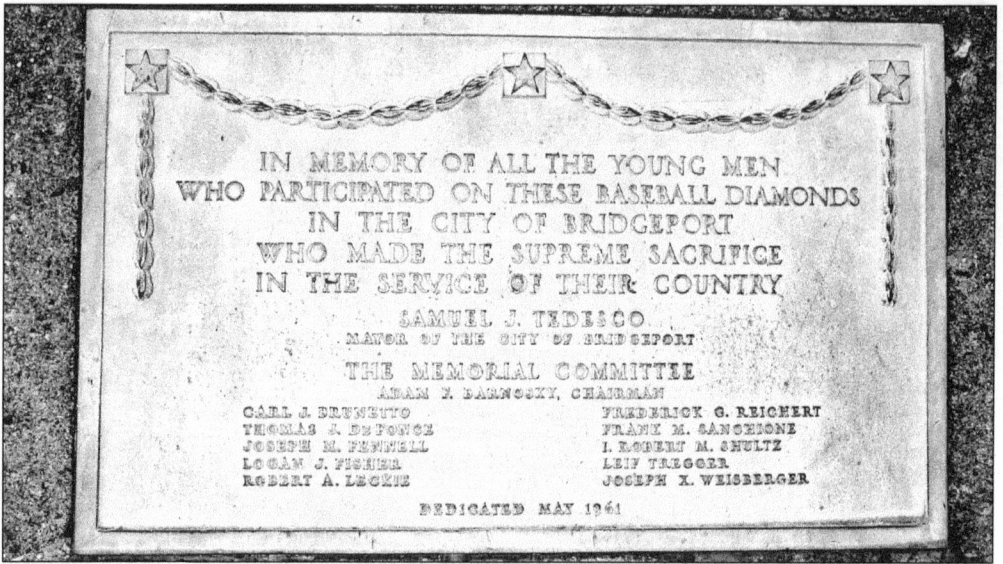

IN MEMORY OF ALL THE YOUNG MEN
WHO PARTICIPATED ON THESE BASEBALL DIAMONDS
IN THE CITY OF BRIDGEPORT
WHO MADE THE SUPREME SACRIFICE
IN THE SERVICE OF THEIR COUNTRY

SAMUEL J. TEDESCO
MAYOR OF THE CITY OF BRIDGEPORT

THE MEMORIAL COMMITTEE
ADAM F. BARNOSKY, CHAIRMAN

CARL J. BRUNETTO   FREDERICK G. REICHERT
THOMAS J. DEFONCE   FRANK M. SANGIONE
JOSEPH M. FENNELL   I. ROBERT M. SHULTZ
LOGAN J. FISHER   LEIF TREGGER
ROBERT A. LECKIE   JOSEPH X. WEISBERGER

DEDICATED MAY 1961

REMEMBERING BRIDGEPORT'S FALLEN BALLPLAYERS. Since 1944, the Senior City Baseball League had planned on erecting a flagpole and monument honoring baseball players of Seaside who gave their lives in the service of their country. On Memorial Day 1961, the touching ceremony at Diamond No. 1 included prayers, songs, and an address by Sen. Prescott Bush. Adam Barnosky was chairman of the league's memorial committee and was also in charge of arrangements.

BRIDGEPORT'S 21ST-CENTURY BASEBALL LOBBY. During summer months, visiting Atlantic League team buses are a customary site at Bridgeport's Holiday Inn on Main Street. Just a few blocks north of the Ballpark at Harbor Yard, the hotel accommodates managers, players, their families, and fans. (Illustration courtesy of Holiday Inn, compliments of Connecticut's Costal Fairfield County Convention and Visitor Bureau.)

Three

BECOMING AMERICA

THE CUBAN (AND ALMOST BRIDGEPORT) GIANTS. Many early black teams half-heartedly disguised their racial identity by attaching the modifier Cuban to their club's name. Placing dollars before racism, the Eastern League invited the popular African American Cuban Giants to join the circuit in late July 1887. It was hoped the Cuban Giants would fill a void created by the departure of New Haven and Bridgeport teams and would play their home games in Bridgeport. The team, however, declined, because barnstorming proved more lucrative. (Photograph courtesy of National Baseball Hall of Fame Library, Cooperstown, New York.)

Moses Fleetwood Walker Visits the Barnum Grounds. Bridgeport diamonds have always hosted famous ballplayers such as catcher "Fleet" Walker, who is acknowledged as the first African American major-leaguer. He is pictured here in 1884 as a member of the American Association Toledo Blue Stockings, 63 years before Jackie Robinson took the field with the Brooklyn Dodgers. Racism and injuries caused Walker's release at the close of his single major-league season. As a member of Waterbury's Southern New England and Eastern League teams in 1885–1886, Walker frequently played in Bridgeport. (Photograph courtesy of National Baseball Hall of Fame Library, Cooperstown, New York.)

HARRY HERBERT, THE FIRST AFRICAN AMERICAN TO PLAY FOR A PROFESSIONAL BRIDGEPORT TEAM. Born c. 1867, Harry Herbert grew up on State Street in Bridgeport. His father was a carpenter, and his mother was a "dyptheria doctress." Herbert started his professional career in 1894 with Pawtucket, and progressive-minded James O'Rourke signed Herbert in 1895 to play with the Victors. Over the course of his four-year professional career in Bridgeport, Herbert batted a solid .289.

HARRY HERBERT, GUITAR-PLAYING OUTFIELDER. During his baseball career, Harry Herbert supported himself as a professional musician. Guitarist Harry Herbert is pictured here on the far left with part of the Jerome May Orchestra c. 1900. The group was one of Bridgeport's most popular dance bands. Herbert was also a founding member of the Bridgeport Social Musical Club in 1905. (Photograph courtesy of Historical Collections, Bridgeport Public Library.)

THE COLUMBIA BASEBALL CLUB, BRIDGEPORT'S 1909 ITALIAN TEAM. Immigrants found that baseball not only provided sport and exercise but also helped preserve their cultural identity while they were becoming accustomed to their new American homes. This is one of several ethnic teams that flourished in Bridgeport.

FULL-BLOODED AMERICAN GIRLS. Long before women regularly participated in organized sports, these workers at the Batcheller Corset factory challenged the norm with a Sunday afternoon of baseball. Enjoying a postgame lunch in their baseball togs are, from left to right, Margaret Heeney, Margaret Maloney, Mabel Katuska, Esther Noden, Anna Kallakatara, and Lucille Miller. A 1911 *Bridgeport Herald* article assured readers that these women were not suffragists and that the pail pictured here was filled with lemonade and not beer.

WILLIAM TIN "BUCK" LAI, BRIDGEPORT'S
FIRST ASIAN PLAYER. Born *c.* 1894 in
Honolulu, Buck Lai was one of 11 children
of Chinese parents. A natural athlete,
Lai toured with the Hawaiian Chinese
University Nine, representing the University
of Hawaii. The team visited Bridgeport in
1916. Two years later, after being invited
to spring training with the Phillies, he was
in the Park City playing third base for the
Bridgeport Americans. He led the Eastern
League in stolen bases during the shortened
1918 season. After the Eastern League, Lai
played several seasons with the independent
Brooklyn Bushwicks. After the 1927 World
Series, Ruth and Gehrig barnstormed as the
Bustin' Babes and Larrupin' Lous. When they
visited the Bushwicks, Buck posed with the
Sultan of Swat. (Photograph courtesy
of Mary Lai.)

SPRING TRAINING, 1928. Buck Lai's
determination resulted in another shot at the
majors. In his early 30s, Buck still exhibited
skills that attracted the attention of Giants
manager John McGraw, who signed the flashy
third baseman to a spring training contract.
(Photograph courtesy of Mary Lai.)

43

BUCK LAI AND THE GEORGIA PEACH. During the Giants' swing south in the spring of 1928, Buck had the opportunity to talk baseball with Ty Cobb, one of the greatest hitters of all time. Cobb, an unabashed bigot, evidently warmed to the Chinese infielder. It was said the Georgia Peach shared batting secrets with Lai. (Photograph courtesy of Mary Lai.)

ANDY YAMASHIRO. Yamashiro played center field for the University of Hawaii team that visited Newfield Park in 1916. Playing under the name Andy Yim, the Japanese-American outfielder from Hawaii was signed by Bridgeport Americans manager Krichell two years later. In this photograph, Yamashiro is posing in Newfield Park. (Photograph from the *Bridgeport Herald*, June 30, 1918.)

HAVANA HEAT. Cuban-born Jose Rodriquez appeared in 58 games with the New York Giants from 1916 to 1918. Returning to the minors, he was Bridgeport's standout infielder during the early 1920s. Playing first and third base, he was a fan favorite who left Bridgeport in the middle of the decade but returned for the 1928–1929 season. Cubans Ramon "Mike" Herrera and screwballer Silvino Ruiz also played with Bridgeport in the 1920s as well as starring in the Negro Leagues.

THE PARK CITY GIANTS, C. 1925. One of Bridgeport's most enduring African American baseball teams was the semiprofessional Park City Giants. Managed by sports enthusiast Bobby Green (pictured in jacket and tie), the Park City Giants won a championship cup in Meriden in 1923. Ace pitcher Edward Bridgeforth is seen in the back row on the far left. (Photograph courtesy of Frank Bridgeforth.)

BRIDGEPORT EMBRACES THE RABBI OF SWAT. Morris Hirsch Solomon's 49 home runs in the Southwestern League in 1923 led the Giants to purchase "the Jewish Babe Ruth." Debuting late that year, Moe played in just two games. In 1924, he split time with four minor-league teams in Toledo, Pittsfield, and Waterbury. From May through August, the Rabbi of Swat played with the Bridgeport Bears. A local paper proclaimed Mose an unsung hero in Bridgeport. (Photograph from the Brace Collection, courtesy of Jewish Major Leaguers Inc.)

"HARRY THE HORSE" DANNING. Baseball was inevitably breaking barriers of ignorance and prejudice. Although not the first Jewish ballplayer from a Bridgeport minor-league team to make the majors, Harry Danning is probably the best known. After duty with the Bridgeport Bears in 1931 and 1932, he went up the minor-league ladder and eventually debuted with the 1933 New York Giants. The same year, Hank Greenberg became the regular left fielder for the Detroit Tigers. Danning, an All-Star catcher, attained a lifetime .285 batting average. (Photograph courtesy of National Baseball Hall of Fame Library, Cooperstown, New York.)

46

THE HERO IN CENTER FIELD. Betty Wilson wanted to play baseball, and the 16-year-old outfielder was allowed to join the all-male 1935 Bronson-Hawley American League team but could only participate in nonleague games. During the summer of 1936, she patrolled Bridgeport center fields with Park Gardens of the Park City League.

RUFUS BAKER, NEGRO LEAGUE STAR. "Scoop" Baker (1918–1992) was born in Atlanta and moved to Connecticut as a boy. He played baseball at Roger Ludlowe High School in Fairfield and was later an infielder for the Bridgeport Colored Stars. Negro League teams visiting Schwarz Field were impressed by Baker's defensive skills. Signed by the Negro National League New York Black Yankees, he was their shortstop from 1943 to 1950. (Photograph courtesy of Craig Kelly.)

THE 1942 BRIDGEPORT COLORED STARS. The semiprofessional Colored Stars played barnstorming Negro League teams at Schwarz Field on River Street. Opponents included the New York Black Yankees, Chicago American Giants, and the Baltimore Elite Giants. The Colored Stars' business manager was Ike Forrest. Rufus Baker was the team's standout infielder. Pictured, from left to right, are the following: (front row) Theherne (first base), Baker (third base), Anderson (right field), Forrest (manager), Jackson (pitcher), Moore (utility), and Scott (utility); (back row) Kelly (catcher), Simms (coach), Wright (second base), Coleman (left field), Collins (shortstop), Shelton (pitcher), and Newkirk (pitcher). (Photograph courtesy of Donnie Forrest.)

DIAMOND GIRLS. World War II again had women marching into Bridgeport factories. Labor and participation in sports provided another step for women in the long road to equality. Here, Blanche Blaskewicz (Blasky) is out by a mile as she rounds third during a 1944 practice game with the GE Ladies Electronics Section team. (Photograph courtesy of Janet Fisher.)

THE GE WOMEN'S TEAM. These General Electric employees were one of the first women's teams to play in the company's inter-section league. They played at GE Field, located on Asylum Street near the back of the Boston Avenue plant, with Bill Mosseau as coach. (Photograph courtesy of Janet Fisher.)

WEDDING BELLS AND BATS AT CANDLELITE STADIUM. On July 1, 1948, Jose Blanco, the Bridgeport Bees' Cuban shortstop, married his childhood sweetheart Margarita Torres in a ballpark ceremony before 1,200 fans. A white carpet was stretched from home plate halfway to the mound, where a justice of the peace waited. After the couple exchanged vows, they walked beneath crossed bats held aloft by the Bees and visiting Poughkeepsie Chiefs. (Photograph by Ed Brinsko, courtesy of the Brinsko family.)

GEORGE HANDY. Signed in 1949, Handy was the first African American to play on a professional Bridgeport team since Harry Herbert in 1898. The second baseman was a member of the Negro League Memphis Red Sox and Houston Eagles before joining the Bees. That year, Handy batted .346 with 22 homers and 25 steals. (Photograph courtesy of Jim Paules.)

BUBBER EVERLASTING. Cowan "Bubber" Hyde, known for his swiftness on the base paths, began his career in the Negro Leagues in 1927. During the summer of 1949, he found himself playing left field at Candlelite Stadium. At the age of 41, he batted .327. (Photograph courtesy of Bridgeport Bluefish.)

THE ORIGINAL BO. Catcher James "Bo" Wallace played in the Negro Leagues with the 1948 Newark Eagles and the 1949 Houston Eagles. In 1950, Bo was a catcher-outfielder for the Bridgeport Bees and led the team in hitting with a .303 average before the Colonial League collapsed in July. Drafted during the Korean War, Bo spent 1951–1952 in military service. His baseball career abruptly ended when he lost most of his left middle finger in a grenade explosion, after which he received the Silver Star and Purple Heart.

REMEMBERING JACKIE. Just hours before game one of the 1997 World Series, Bo Wallace returned to Bridgeport as part of Bridgeport Public Library's 50th-anniversary celebration of Jackie Robinson breaking the major-league color barrier. Mayor Joseph Ganim officially proclaimed Saturday, October 18, 1997, as Bo Wallace Day. The former Bridgeport Bee is pictured here holding the mayor's proclamation while adoring fans at the Newfield Branch Library look on.

BEE IN THE HIVE ONCE AGAIN. Bo Wallace would return to Bridgeport one last time. Here, the old catcher throws out the ceremonial first pitch for the Bridgeport Bluefish on opening day, May 5, 1999. Never bitter, always the gentleman, Wallace passed away in 2000. Bridgeport will miss his warm gravel voice and broad smile. (Photograph courtesy of Bridgeport Bluefish)

Four

AT THE HELM IN BRIDGEPORT

BRIDGEPORT'S FIRST PROFESSIONAL MANAGER. Bridgeport entered baseball's professional ranks in 1885. The manager of the Southern New England League Bridgeport Giants was Bridgeport-born Dan Shannon. The Giants left the SNEL to join the Eastern League in August 1885. The next year, Shannon managed Newburyport. In 1887, he returned to take the reins of Bridgeport's Eastern League club. Shannon (standing on the far left) is pictured here when he was the second baseman and manager of the 1889 American Association Louisville Colonels. (Photograph courtesy of National Baseball Hall of Fame Library, Cooperstown, New York.)

UNCLE JEEMS. From 1895 to 1909, Orator Jim O'Rourke was the player-manager-owner of the city's professional club—one team, three successive names: the Victors, Soubrettes, and Orators. With Bridgeport, O'Rourke appeared in 913 games, had 3,517 at bats, and hit .301. During the 15 years he owned the Bridgeport team, he managed all but 12 of their games. O'Rourke's managerial record stands at 734 wins, 722 losses, and 18 ties resulting in a .504 winning percentage. Later in life, the ever-popular ballplayer was affectionately dubbed Uncle Jeems. Orator Jim is the grand old man of Bridgeport baseball! (Photograph courtesy of Historical Collections, Bridgeport Public Library.)

MCCANN AND THE MECHANICS. O'Rourke sold his team in February 1910 to H. Eugene McCann. McCann, a minor-league pitcher and former Jersey City manager, was also a scout for the New York Highlanders. He sponsored a contest in April 1910 to rename the team, and a committee of Bridgeport sportswriters chose "the Mechanics." McCann managed Bridgeport until June 1913. He led New London to a pennant in 1914 and eventually returned to manage the Bridgeport Americans from 1921 to 1923. (Photograph courtesy of Historical Collections, Bridgeport Public Library.)

MONTE CROSS, 1913. Cross was named Bridgeport's manager by owner John H. Freeman on June 16, 1913. For the remainder of the season, the team was affectionately nicknamed the Crossmen and finished the campaign in fourth place. Cross had played 15 years in the majors, mostly with the National League Philadelphia Phillies and American League Philadelphia Athletics. Before being hired by Bridgeport, Cross was an Eastern Association umpire. (Photograph courtesy of National Baseball Hall of Fame Library, Cooperstown, New York.)

MONTE CROSS
SHORTSTOP OF THE PHILADELPHIA (A. L.) CLUB OF 1902

JAKE BOULTES, 1914. This Mechanics third baseman holds the distinction of being arrested for playing baseball. In 1913, Sunday games were against state law, and Boultes was playing baseball at Newfield on that very day. The case was dismissed when the witness misidentified Boultes in the crowded courtroom. Boultes became manager the next season and brought the Eastern Association Bridgeport Bolts to a respectable third-place finish.

55

NEAL BALL, SECOND BASEMAN AND MANAGER, 1916. There was no professional ball in Bridgeport during 1915. When Bridgeport resident Neal Ball was traded from Toronto it was his ill luck to inherit the dismal 1916 Bridgeport Hustlers. Struggling to stay out of last place, Ball was relieved of duty in July.

BALL MAKES HISTORY. On July 19, 1909, Ball was playing shortstop for the Cleveland Naps against the visiting Boston Red Sox. Boston had two runners on with no outs in the top of the second inning. Ball caught a line drive by McConnell, touched second base to double up Wagner, and then tagged Stahl running from first base. There it was, the first unassisted major-league triple play. In the bottom of the inning, Ball hit an inside-the-park home run. Shown in this photograph are, from left to right, Amby McConnell, Neal Ball, Heinie Wagner, and Jake Stahl.

56

PAUL KRICHELL, 1917–1918. This reserve catcher for the St. Louis Browns never hit a home run but would eventually make a major impact on baseball. Krichell successfully managed the Bridgeport Americans for a season and a half until he resigned in June 1918, when the Eastern League took away two victories from Bridgeport. Krichell became the Red Sox coach in 1919. In 1920, Krichell was hired as a Yankee scout by general manager Ed Barrow. The former Bridgeport skipper was responsible for signing most of the 1927 Yankee infield, which included Gehrig, Koenig, and Lazzeri. He also discovered Hall of Fame Yankee pitcher Whitey Ford. (Photograph courtesy of National Baseball Hall of Fame Library, Cooperstown, New York.)

THE BROTHERS GRIMES. First baseman Ray Grimes replaced Krichell and remained as manager until the Eastern League "cracked" on July 22, 1918, due to the U.S. government's World War I work-or-fight edict. During the 1919 season, three Grimes brothers—twins Ray and Roy along with Kenneth—played together for the Bridgeport Americans. Ray, pictured here with the Cubs, batted .354 for Chicago in 1922. (Photograph courtesy of National Baseball Hall of Fame Library, Cooperstown, New York.)

HALL OF FAMER "BIG ED" WALSH, 1920. The former Chicago White Sox great, pictured here in his Americans uniform, led the 1920 Bridgeport club to a fifth-place finish. Unpopular in the clubhouse, Walsh was accused of tactical miscues and riding players too hard. The spitballer's 1.82 ERA compiled after 14 seasons makes him the all-time ERA leader. He was elected to the Hall of Fame in 1946. (Photograph from the *Bridgeport Evening Post*, June 1, 1921.)

DOC HOBLITZEL. The Americans became property of a Springfield, Massachusetts syndicate in January 1924, with former Connecticut League manager Jack O'Hara acting as president and manager. Another contest was held to rename the team, and local sportswriters, considering the city's circus history, decided on "Bears." Later, in 1924, Dick Hoblitzel, dentist and former first baseman for the Reds and Red Sox, took the reins. Ten years earlier, Hoblitzel had been Babe Ruth's roommate while with Boston.

HOBLITZELL, CINCINNATI - NATIONALS

IRVIN "KAISER" WILHELM, 1925.
Kise broke into the majors as a
right-handed pitcher with the 1903
Pirates. Pittsburgh won the National
League championship that year, and
although Wilhelm did not face the
Boston Pilgrims in the postseason,
it marked the birth of the modern
World Series. George Stallings and
Walter Hapgood brought Kaiser to
Bridgeport in 1925, the same year the
Bears finished two games below .500
in sixth place. (Photograph courtesy of
National Baseball Hall of Fame Library,
Cooperstown, New York.)

BUD STAPLETON, ONCE AND FUTURE MANAGER, 1926–1927 AND 1932. Bears fans celebrated
Bud Stapleton Day on August 23, 1926, at Newfield Park. Stapleton is shown sitting at the
wheel of his surprise gift while the visiting Springfield Ponies stand behind the Chrysler. Ponies
manager and former Bridgeport manager Gene McCann is standing fourth from the left while
Bridgeport Mayor F. William Behrens, standing on the far right, is holding a straw hat. Bud
returned as manager in 1932 but saw little playing time due to blood poisoning he suffered in a
spring training injury. The Great Depression caused the Eastern League to collapse in July 1932.
(Photograph courtesy of Historical Collections, Bridgeport Public Library.)

FIRST WITH THE BEARS, SECOND TO A HORSE. An outstanding pre–World War I third baseman, Hans Lobert coached at West Point from 1918 to 1925. In 1929, the New York Giants acquired the Bears as their Eastern League farm club and named Lobert as manager. He took the club to second place, and the Bears finished first in the second half of the 1930 split season. This was the first time since 1904 that Bridgeport was involved in a championship. During Lobert's playing days, his speed was legendary. In 1913, he was challenged to race a horse around the bases. He lost only in the last moment when the horse crowded him rounding second. (Photograph courtesy of National Baseball Hall of Fame Library, Cooperstown, New York.)

RUDY HULSWIT, 1941. Hulswit actually broke into the majors in 1899, when he played one game with the National League Louisville Colonels. He managed the 1941 Inter-State Bridgeport Bees until August of that year when he was reassigned as a scout. Pitcher Charlie Suche was appointed "temporary" skipper. It would be the Baby Bees' only season in Bridgeport. (Photograph courtesy of National Baseball Hall of Fame Library, Cooperstown, New York.)

CARL BRUNETTO AND THE TEAM WITH NO NAME, 1947. For years, sports enthusiast Brunetto was involved with local baseball. He managed Senior City League clubs as well as promoted Negro League visits under the lights at Schwarz Field. His dream came true when he became co-owner of Bridgeport's Class B Colonial League club. Career minor-leaguer Mike Sabena had been introduced as Bridgeport's new manager, but it was Carl Brunetto who took the helm at the start of 1947. Brunetto's fiery temperament was well known and would lead to a succession of field generals. Bridgeport's club went an entire year without a name, and the Class B Colonial League entry was only identified as "Bridgeport" in the sports page throughout their inaugural 1947 season. It was not until 1948 that the team was dubbed the Bees. Brunetto (left), who enjoyed going nose to nose with umpires, is pictured here with his mentor Leo Durocher at the Hotel Taft in New Haven. (Photograph courtesy of Duke Sherwood and family.)

OLLIE BYERS, 1949. Byers joined the parade of Bridgeport managers in 1949. The Bridgeport Bees Booster Club honored former Boston Braves star and future Hall of Famer Rabbit Maranville along with new manager Byers at a sold-out Candlelite Restaurant dinner that February. From left to right are an unidentified boy, Rabbit Maranville, an unidentified boy, and Ollie Byers. Byers during the spring told reporters he had never been fired. Brunetto changed that on August 1. (Photograph courtesy of Duke Sherwood and family.)

FRANK SILVA, 1949. While the search
for a skipper was under way, general
manager Frank Silva, who arrived in
late 1948, temporarily piloted the Bees
during the first week of August 1949.
He is standing just outside the players'
clubhouse at Candlelite. (Photograph
courtesy of Jim Paules.)

DOUBLE X IN BRIDGEPORT, 1949. Jimmie Foxx, the
former American League slugger, was signed as Bees
emergency manager in early August 1949. Initially,
it was agreed Foxx would remain with the team
until Rabbit Maranville took over. Business matters
forced Maranville to change his decision, and Foxx
remained as manager from August 6 to 19, 1949, after
which he was called home due to his wife's illness.
(Photograph courtesy of Bridgeport Bluefish.)

JIMMIE FOXX FIELD. During his brief 1949 stay, Jimmie Foxx took time to chat with some Bridgeport boys at a local park. Two years later, his .325 lifetime batting average and 534 homers earned Foxx a place in Cooperstown. (Photograph courtesy of Duke Sherwood and family.)

JIM PAULES, 1949. When Jimmie Foxx left Bridgeport to take part in an old-timers' game at Yankee Stadium honoring Connie Mack, popular Bees first baseman Dutch Paules managed the team (August 20–22, 1949). When Foxx returned home to Pennsylvania for good, Tom Downey piloted the club for the remainder of the 1949 season. (Photograph courtesy of Jim Paules.)

BUD'S BACK, 1950. Stapleton returned in 1950 to become manager during another league collapse. A split season format was instituted in 1950 with the Bridgeport Bees finishing the first half in fifth place (out of six teams). They lost the first seven games entering the second half before the Class B Colonial League dissolved on July 14, 1950. (Photograph courtesy of Jim Paules.)

BRIDGEPORT'S FIRST PROFESSIONAL MANAGER IN ALMOST HALF A CENTURY. The city's baseball legacy was revived by the new independent Atlantic League Bridgeport Bluefish. Willie Upshaw, former player and coach for the Toronto Blue Jays, was the first Bluefish manager (1998–2000). In their inaugural season, Bridgeport won both halves of the split season but lost to Atlantic City in the Championship Series. The Bluefish responded by taking the Atlantic League Crown in 1999. It was the 95th anniversary of the last time Bridgeport won a league championship. (Photograph courtesy of Bridgeport Bluefish.)

MIRACLE MET DUFFY DYER. Duffy Dyer was Bluefish manager for 2001–2002. Under his guidance, Bridgeport captured the Atlantic League's North Division in both the first and second halves of 2002 but lost to the Newark Bears in the Championship Series. As a catcher, Dyer spent his first seven years with the New York Mets and was a member of the 1969 world champions and the 1973 "Ya Gotta Believe" team. In February 2003, he became an advance scout for the Mets. (Photograph courtesy of Bridgeport Bluefish.)

JOSE LIND. On February 27, 2003, Lind became the third manager in Bluefish history. He played in the majors from 1987 to 1995 and won a Gold Glove with Pittsburgh in 1992. The second baseman arrived in Bridgeport during the team's 1999 Atlantic League championship drive. His best season as a Bluefish player occurred in 2000, when he was selected to the Atlantic League All-Star team. Lind served as a bench coach until being named Bluefish manager. (Photograph courtesy of Bridgeport Bluefish.)

Five

LINEUPS

THE BRIDGEPORT FRIENDLY UNITED SOCIAL CLUB (TBFUS). Commonly referred to as the TBs, they were one of Bridgeport's amateur teams during the 1870s and 1880s. James "Chief" Roseman went on to a major-league career with several teams, including the American Association New York Metropolitans. John O'Rourke, brother of James, was also a TB member. From April 1875 to April 1876, he served as a city councilman during Mayor P.T. Barnum's administration. (Illustration from the *Bridgeport Post*, September 4, 1934.)

BRIDGEPORT'S STAR CENTER FIELDER. Jimmy Ryan is pictured here (first row, far left) while a member of the 1884 Hudson, Massachusetts team. A year later, he would be the star center fielder for the Bridgeport Giants. By season's end, he was with Cap Anson's National League Chicago White Stockings. Ryan would play more than 2,000 major-league games and achieve 2,556 hits with a .311 lifetime average. (Photograph courtesy of National Baseball Hall of Fame Library, Cooperstown, New York.)

A LONG WAY FROM BRIDGEPORT. During the winter of 1888–1889, former Bridgeport outfielder and current White Stockings player Jim Ryan was a member of baseball's historic world tour. Organized by White Stockings owner Albert G. Spalding, Chicago played games against their traveling opponents, a hand-picked team called the All-Americans. On February 9, 1889, the squads visited the Sphinx, played a game in the shadow of the Pyramids, and posed for this photograph. Afterward, players attempted to throw baseballs over the Pyramids and targeted the right eye of the Sphinx. (Photograph courtesy of National Baseball Hall of Fame Library, Cooperstown, New York.)

CONNECTICUT'S CONNIE MACK. Mr. Mack began his 66-year professional baseball career as a catcher for Meriden in 1884. The following season, as a member of the Hartford team, he played at the Barnum Grounds against the Southern New England League Bridgeport Giants. During 1885, Mack employed a rubber catching pad invented by a teammate to soften the impact of the pitcher's delivery. Otherwise, he was fond of placing a slice of steak into the palm of his thin glove. (Photograph courtesy of Transcendental Graphics.)

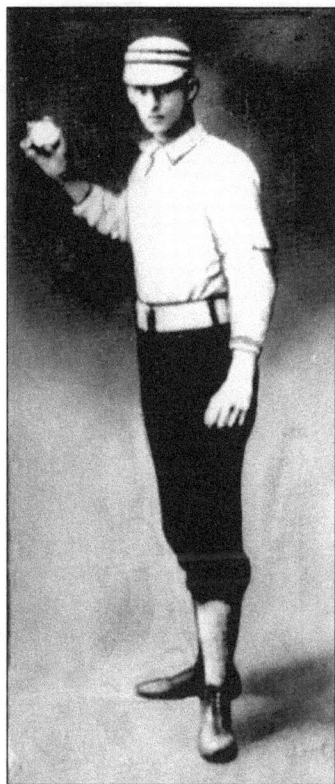

MR. MACK MAINTAINS BRIDGEPORT TIES. In 1901, Connie Mack embarked upon his 50-year reign as manager (and eventual sole owner) of the American League Philadelphia Athletics. Mack would bring his Athletics to play exhibition games at Newfield Park. While managing Philadelphia, he never wore a uniform in the dugout, opting instead for a shirt and tie. A half-century of ball fans would never forget his familiar pose, positioning players with the wave of his scorecard. (Photograph courtesy of National Baseball Hall of Fame Library, Cooperstown, New York.)

BILLY ALVORD. "Uncle Billy" Alvord arrived in Bridgeport when he was 22 years old. He played with the Eastern League Bridgeport Giants from late May until the end of September 1886. The previous year, he went hitless in two games with the National League St. Louis Maroons. Alvord finished his major-league career in Cleveland with the 1893 Spiders. (Photograph courtesy of Transcendental Graphics.)

JACK MCMAHON. Catcher Jack McMahon batted .313 in the four games he played with the 1887 Bridgeport Giants. The Bridgeport resident bounced around in the minors until making the New York Giant teams of 1892–1893. He died just two years afterward at the age of 25. This photograph was taken by Seeley and Warnock in Bridgeport. (Photograph courtesy of National Baseball Hall of Fame Library, Cooperstown, New York.)

BRIDGEPORT'S GIANT. Thomas Lovett, pitcher for the Bridgeport Giants in 1887, attained a 21-3 record while striking out 170 batters in 217 innings. He led the league in strikeouts, winning percentage (.875), and ERA (1.12). Lovett powered Bridgeport to the first half Eastern League Championship, but the team disbanded prior to the second half. He eventually played in the postseason with Brooklyn in the 1889 and 1890 World Series and faced James O'Rourke of the New York Giants during the 1889 World Series. The Orator smoked a double and a home run off Lovett in the second inning of game seven in the best-of-nine contest. Lovett is pictured here as a member of the 1894 Boston Beaneaters. (Photograph courtesy of Transcendental Graphics.)

WILLIAM GARONI. Garoni pitched one season for the 1899 Bridgeport Orators, and he started 26 games and completed all but three. His five shutouts and 9-13 record impressed the New York Giants. The National League club signed Garoni, and his major-league debut came on September 7, 1899. He would pitch only two more games for New York that year, retiring with a lifetime 0-1 record. This photograph shows Garoni pitching for Fort Lee, New Jersey. (Photograph courtesy of National Baseball Hall of Fame Library, Cooperstown, New York.)

THE BEST TEAM TO PLAY AT NEWFIELD PARK. The Orators won the 1904 pennant, making them the only league championship team to call Newfield Park their home. Despite late-season injuries, the Orators still established a new Connecticut League record with 71 wins, and the .275 team batting average was outstanding for the dead ball era. However, controversy clouded the season. New Haven had finished on top of the league but only because action was not taken regarding their use of suspended pitcher Thomas Tuckey. A vote by league directors on November 15, 1904, legally bound New Haven to forfeit the games of August 1 against Norwich and August 5 against Bridgeport. The decision awarded Bridgeport the 1904 Championship. (Photograph from *Spalding's Official Base Ball Guide 1905*, courtesy of Stephen Milman.)

BRIDGEPORT'S POP. Clarence "Pop" Foster was the star of the 1904 Orators, leading the Connecticut League in hits (158), doubles (33), triples (15), and batting (.376). Previously he had played major-league ball with the Giants, Washington Senators, and White Sox from 1898 to 1901.

FOR THE LOVE OF SPORTS. After a career in minor-league ball, Foster turned to coaching athletics at schools and colleges, including NYU, Mercersburg Academy, and Bridgeport High School. During World War I, he served as an athletic director for the army with the rank of captain. Pop coached Princeton University's wrestling team from 1924 to 1934. He remained with Princeton's physical education department until his death in 1944. In this view, Foster is seated on the far left with the 1924–1925 wrestling team. (Photograph courtesy of Princeton University Library.)

MCCANN'S MECHANICS. Eugene McCann bought the Orators from James O'Rourke in February 1910 for $7,500, and the team's name was changed. On opening day in 1910, the Bridgeport Mechanics traveled to Savin Rock and defeated New Haven 3-1. It was the Mechanics' first-ever regular season game. The Mechanics ended the year in second place. (Photograph courtesy of Historical Collections, Bridgeport Public Library.)

HUGH DUFFY. The Victors first game of 1896 was an April 12 exhibition game against the National League Boston Beaneaters at Bridgeport's Athletic Park. Five hundred cranks (what are now called fans) watched future Hall of Fame outfielder Hugh Duffy score four runs for the Beaneaters that afternoon. Years later, Duffy would return to Bridgeport on a regular basis as owner-manager of the 1916 Eastern League Portland Duffs. (Photograph courtesy of Transcendental Graphics.)

GAMBLING. The *Bridgeport Daily Standard* noted in 1886, "Gambling and intemperance should be closely suppressed by the managers [of the Eastern League] if it is desired that the games be attended by the better class of people." The article does not state if gambling was problematic in the stands or clubhouse. This *c.* 1910 betting slip lists Connecticut League as well as major-league teams. Bettors were gambling on runs scored during a given week. In 1920, workers at Newfield Park announced they would not answer telephones during game time. Savvy gamblers wagering on inning-by-inning results were swamping the ticket office with calls. In this manner, they hoped to get scores and bet before runs were announced across news tickertapes.

A BASEBALL GAME SLIP.

HIRSUTE HITTERS AND HURLERS. The exceptionally talented, if somewhat peculiar, House of David baseball team toured the country and visited Newfield Park during the 1930s and 1940s. Hailing from Benton Harbor, Michigan, this popular touring team was actually part of a religious colony led by Ohio farmer Benjamin Purell. Members were not allowed to cut their hair, hence the flowing waist-length locks and beards. (Photograph courtesy of Clara Janus.)

THE BRIDGEPORT BOLTS, 1914. First-year manager and third baseman Jack Boultes piloted the Eastern Association Bridgeport Bolts to a third-place finish in 1914 behind New London and Waterbury. Billy Hallman led the team in batting with a .294 average, and Bobby Stow led the league in stolen bases with 71. In May 1914, Newfield Park was the setting for a silent baseball film, and members of the Bolts were used as extras. Manager Boultes is shown in this photograph in the second row, fourth from the left.

"SILENT JOHN" GILLESPIE SPEAKS VOLUMES AT BAT. Pitcher Gillespie played professional ball for eight years, including one season with the 1922 Cincinnati Reds. He finished that year with a record of 3-3. He batted .133 and hit no home runs. That would all change on August 9, 1923, when, hurling for the Bridgeport Americans in Springfield against the Ponies, Gillespie became the only pitcher to hit four home runs in one professional baseball game. This record was discovered by Bob McConnell. (Photograph courtesy of Chicago Historical Society.)

LOU GEHRIG AS LOU LEWIS. During his minor-league days with the Hartford Senators (1921, 1923–1924), Lou Gehrig often played at Newfield Park. During his first year in Hartford, he played under the assumed name "Lou Lewis" so he would not endanger his eligibility to play with Columbia University. In 1924, he batted .369 for the Senators and was called up permanently to the Yankees the following year. Shown in this photograph are Hartford manager and former Yankees coach Patrick "Paddy" O'Connor (left) with his star first baseman. (Photograph courtesy of National Baseball Hall of Fame Library, Cooperstown, New York.)

THE MIRACLE MAN. George Tweedy Stallings was the first manager of the Detroit Tigers. However, he is best remembered as the manager of the 1914 Miracle Braves of Boston. In 1925, Stallings co-owned the Bridgeport Bears. (Photograph courtesy of National Baseball Hall of Fame Library, Cooperstown, New York.)

BEARS IN BRIDGEPORT AND ON WALL STREET. The stock market crash of 1929 devastated minor-league baseball. With so many families unemployed, attending ball games became a low priority. The drop in ticket revenues doomed small market minor-league teams, and split seasons were enacted in 1930 and 1931. Allentown won the first half of 1930, and Bridgeport topped the second. The Allentown Buffaloes defeated the Bears (pictured here) in the Eastern League Championship four games to one.

JO-JO "THE GAUSE GHOST" MOORE. The quick outfielder from Gause, Texas, shuffled between the Giants and teams within their minor-league system. In August 1931, Jo-Jo was shipped to Bridgeport before heading to the Giants permanently in 1932. He had two hits in one inning in the 1933 World Series and played in two more Fall Classics. He was named to five All-Star squads and attained a lifetime .298 batting average. (Photograph courtesy of National Baseball Hall of Fame Library, Cooperstown, New York.)

THE RECIPE FOR SUCCESS. Bridgeport resident George "Kiddo" Davis played eight years in the majors and batted a combined .381 in two World Series with the New York Giants. When Bob Beslove was a child, his neighbor Kiddo Davis told him the recipe for being a good ball player: "Eat a 'mix sweetening' of whole wheat bread and apples." Beslove's school lunches changed immediately. From that day forward, his mom made sandwiches on whole wheat and included an apple for dessert. (Photograph courtesy of National Baseball hall of Fame Library, Cooperstown, New York.)

JOE MALAY. When the 1930 Hartford Senators withdrew from the Eastern League, the Bridgeport Bears purchased the contract of first baseman Joe Malay. His 1930 combined team batting average was .268 with Hartford and Bridgeport and .310 for his next full year with the Bears. When Malay was called up to the Giants, he played in only a handful of games in 1933 and 1935. The Bridgeport resident had the hard luck of playing backup to Hall of Famer Bill Terry. (Photograph courtesy of National Baseball Hall of Fame Library, Cooperstown, New York.)

A SANDLOT HERO. Ray Keating was born in Bridgeport on July 21, 1891. While growing up, he was coached by Richard Mansfield, the former Orator. In 1909, Keating pitched for Bridgeport's St. Charles team in the Park City League. Keating is shown standing fifth from the left. (Scrapbook photograph courtesy of Historical Collections, Bridgeport Public Library.)

RAY KEATING DAY. A highlight of Keating's baseball career came on June 7, 1913, when nearly 2,000 Bridgeport fans traveled by train to New York to cheer their hero. Disembarking at the 125th Street Station, the throng stopped traffic parading to the Eighth Avenue El. At the Polo Grounds (the Giants shared the stadium with the Yankees), the Bridgeport rooters serenaded Ray and presented him with a silver bat, a loving cup, and a huge floral horseshoe. (Illustration from the *Bridgeport Herald*, June 8, 1913.)

BRIDGEPORT'S SPITBALLER. This 1914 blanket shows Park City native Ray Keating of the New York Yankees. At the time, certain tobacco brands issued small felt-type cloth squares portraying popular players. Keating pitched for New York from 1912 to 1916 and again in 1918. His Yankee totals are 24 wins and 40 losses. Ray Keating finished his career with the Boston Braves in 1919 with a 7-11 record.

THE BRIDGEPORT ELKS BASEBALL TEAM, LODGE NO. 36, 1910–1911. One special member of this squad is pitcher Edward T. Buckingham, standing fourth from the left, wearing a Yale Law School uniform. Buckingham was born in Metuchen, New Jersey, on May 12, 1874, and moved to Bridgeport as a child. He appeared in one major-league game on August 30, 1895. Buckingham pitched three innings in the first game of a doubleheader for the Washington Senators. He surrendered five runs on six hits, two walks, and one strikeout against St. Louis. Members of this Elks team are, from left to right, as follows: (front row) Archie McNeil Jr., Thomas Youngs, Ed Dunn, Steve Boucher (city clerk), Harry Johnson, Robert Nichols, and Em Donnelly; (back row) Joseph Lindley, William O'Leary, William Bentley, Edward T. Buckingham, Henry Kane, J.I. Flint, Joseph Dowling, Fritz Musante, Michael J. Flanagan, and Louis Brock. (Photograph courtesy of Historical Collections, Bridgeport Public Library.)

THE KING OF SPORTS, C. 1935. Ed Buckingham was a devoted tennis player and was city champion for several years. The morning after his pitching debut with Washington, August 31, 1895, he was back on Bridgeport courts winning a finals match. Buckingham helped organize the city's baseball Industrial League and served as league president before America's entry into World War I. He served as a member of the board of recreation throughout the 1920s. In 1926, he was elected first president of the Bridgeport Swimming Association. (Photograph courtesy of Historical Collections, Bridgeport Public Library.)

CITIZEN BUCKINGHAM. Ed Buckingham graduated from Yale Law School in 1897 (he also pitched for the Elis) and was elected democratic justice of the peace the following year. He served as city clerk (1901–1909), mayor of Bridgeport for three terms (1909–1911 and 1929–1933), compensation commissioner for Fairfield County, and as a member of Bridgeport's board of education. Bridgeport's politician-athlete died on July 30, 1942. (Photograph courtesy of Historical Collections, Bridgeport Public Library.)

AN ECLECTIC ASSEMBLAGE AT THE BALLPARK, 1940. Shown here are, from left to right, Ed Buckingham; Dennis Carroll, secretary of the hatters' union and member of the Mallory Hat Company team; drum majorette Arlene Hall of the Danbury hatters' union fife and drum corps; Edwin Kane, corps instructor; Dennis Carroll Jr.; and well-known radio comedian Colonel Stoopnagle. They were all on hand for an old-timers' baseball game in Danbury. (Photograph courtesy of Historical Collections, Bridgeport Public Library.)

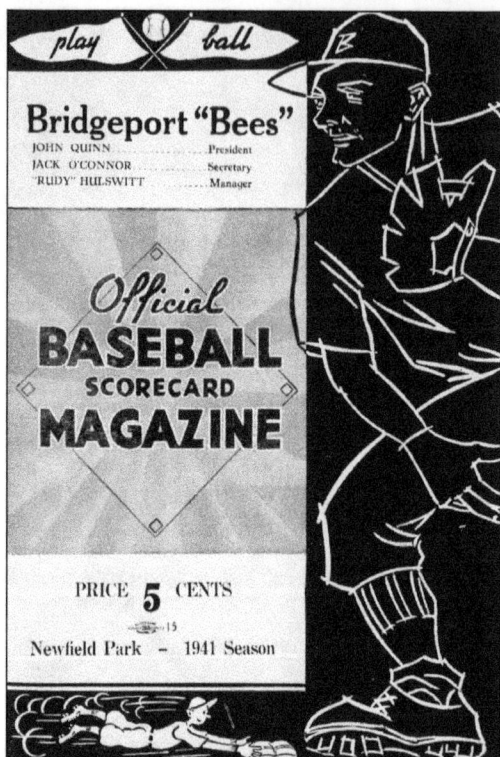

A 1941 BEES SCORECARD. Following Bridgeport's withdrawal from the Eastern League in 1932, the baseball drought lasted eight years. Professional ball was revived in the city when the National League Boston Braves, known as the Bees from 1936 to 1940, transferred their York, Pennsylvania club to Connecticut. The Inter-State League Bees finished second from last, and hopes for another opening day were dashed due to low gate receipts, the military draft, and wartime dim-out rules.

THE 1948 BRIDGEPORT BEES. The Class B Colonial League Bees held spring training in New Bern, North Carolina. From left to right are the following: (front row) Jose Abreu, Arthur Clune, Leo Marcil Jr., Willie Reyes, Walter Collins, and Jose Blanco; (middle row) Emil Malattia, Nat Trout, Bobby Sherwood, Carl Armstrong, William Richardson, and Edward Lennon; (back row) Glenn Snyder, William Grossman, James Hansen, Jack Estes, Fritz Luciano, William Green, and Mel Kaman. (Photograph courtesy of Duke Sherwood and family.)

THE BEES' BEST FAN. Ardent fan Ruth (Farrell) Paules loved to score every Bees game. Once, her scorecard was even entered as the official record. Here, Bobby Sherwood (co-owner and outfielder) presents Ruth with a 1948 season ticket. The photograph was taken at her family's business, the Willis Seed and Bird Store on Fairfield Avenue. Note the framed chickens in the background. (Photograph courtesy of Jim Paules.)

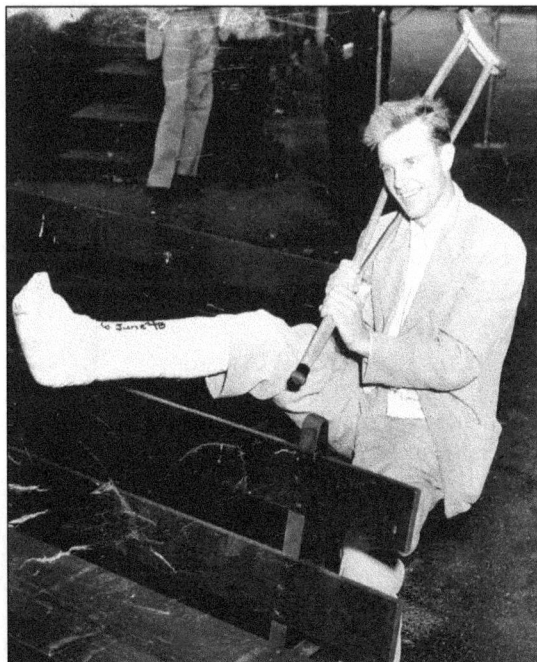

ALWAYS GENIAL. Bobby Sherwood chipped the bone in his right ankle while sliding into third base during a June 6, 1948 game in Port Chester against the Clippers. Bridgeport was in second place at the time, but with Sherwood's bat out of the lineup, the team finished fifth. The Bees' co-owner and center fielder is shown in the stands of Candlelite Stadium a few days after his accident. The writing on the cast notes the date of the injury. (Photograph courtesy of Duke Sherwood and family.)

A BRIDGEPORT BEES OPENING DAY TICKET, 1948. What baseball fan does not have at least one ticket stub tucked away? The stubs are instant pieces of memorabilia linked to an exact place and time. Their faded date and seat number forever hold a summer day. Game tickets are treasured for the memories they create as well as for their artwork. The wonderful design of this opening day Bees ticket dates from the golden age of baseball. (Photograph courtesy of Duke Sherwood and family.)

JIM PAULES'S 1949 MVP CEREMONY. First baseman Jim "Dutch" Paules was honored as the Bees' MVP before the September 5 morning game. It was the last day of the 1949 season, and gifts included luggage, a suit, hat, wristwatch, a camera, and photographs. The MVP vote was conducted by WNAB radio personality Phil Peterson. (Photograph courtesy of Jim Paules.)

Six

THE NIGHT THE CARDINALS
NEARLY DIED

A TERRIBLE JUMBLE. In the wee hours of Tuesday, July 11, 1911, the Federal Express train, running 1 hour and 20 minutes behind schedule, roared into Bridgeport. About a block west of the Fairfield Avenue railroad bridge, the engineer took the switch at 60 miles per hour, where the speed limit was only 15 miles per hour. At 3:35 a.m., Engine 413 jumped the tracks and plunged 18 feet down to street level.

WRECKAGE. A surreal landscape strewn with the dead and injured, remains of splintered railroad cars, and twisted rails all flashed into view with the electrical sparks of downed wires. Twelve were killed and dozens injured. Among the passengers of the Federal Express were members of the St. Louis Cardinals heading north to Boston for a game against the National League Rustlers. The fact that none of the Cardinal players were injured or killed resulted from a quirk of fate. (Photograph courtesy of Historical Collections, Bridgeport Public Library.)

THE BALLPLAYERS' PULLMAN. Originally, the two cars the ballplayers occupied were located near the front of the train. Between Washington and Jersey City, manager Roger Bresnahan complained that his players could not sleep because of the noise from the engine. As a result, the cars were rearranged in the Harlem rail yards, and the day coach, which would be destroyed in the wreck, took the place of one of the Cardinals' Pullman cars. After the tumbling cars came to a rest, the team scrambled from their Pullman, shown here. (Photograph courtesy of Historical Collections, Bridgeport Public Library.)

AN EXHAUSTED RESCUE WORKER. This Bridgeport police officer was one of the many heroes who helped with rescue efforts on July 11, 1911. Twenty-two members of the Cardinal organization on board the Federal Express train were the very first to assist surviving passengers. They are Miller Huggins, Joe Hauser, Mike Mowrey, Ed Konetchy, H.F. Sallee, Bob Harmon, Bill Steele, Roy Golden, Jack Bliss, Rube Ellis, Steve Evans, Rebel Oakes, Roger Bresnahan, Otto McIvor, Jack McAdams, Lee Magee, Ivey Wingo, Wally Smith, Grover Lowdermilk, Louie Lowdermilk, Rube Geyer, and Secretary Seekamp. (Photograph courtesy of Historical Collections, Bridgeport Public Library.)

Within the photograph, handwritten:

St. Louis National Base Ball Team on
top overturned Pullman Wreck, Federal
Express, Bridgeport, Conn. July 11 - 1911.
Duplicates at Jacksons.

HEROES OFF THE FIELD. The *Bridgeport Daily Standard* reported, "Under the personal leadership of Manager Roger Bresnahan [the] scantily attired [St. Louis ballplayers] did heroic work in rescuing the injured. Many of those imprisoned in the overturned Pullmans were assisted to safety by them." This photograph, taken later in the day on July 11, 1911, shows members of the St. Louis Cardinals posing on the wreckage. From left to right are the following: (front row) Joe Hauser, unidentified, unidentified, Rebel Oakes, and Roger Bresnahan; (back row) unidentified, unidentified, Ivey Wingo, Jack Bliss, Grover Lowdermilk, unidentified, Ed Konetchy, and unidentified. (Photograph courtesy of Historical Collections, Bridgeport Public Library.)

Seven

WHEN BASEBALL
RULED BRIDGEPORT

UNION METALLIC CARTRIDGE, INDUSTRIAL LEAGUE, 1908. During the summer of 1908, the Union Typewriter (Yost) Company defeated Union Metallic Cartridge twice, both times in 12 innings. Anticipation ran high in the city when a special Labor Day playoff game was needed. The *Bridgeport Telegram* reported "considerable money" changed hands among the 2,000 fans at Newfield Park, which saw Union Metallic Cartridge defeat Union Typewriter 8-1. Union Metallic Cartridge was awarded the Kinder Cup and a huge pennant created by the Howland Dry Goods Company. (Photograph courtesy of Historical Collections, Bridgeport Public Library.)

BASEBALL'S MR. COFFEY. Jack Coffey was an outstanding pitcher with the 1908 Union Metallic Cartridge champions. A Park City version of "Casey at the Bat," albeit with a happier ending, appeared in a local paper. One portion of "Jack Coffey in the Box" reads, "All of life's emotions come trooping on in flocks, when we see the striker smash the air, with Jack Coffey in the box."

THE BIG TRAIN PULLS INTO BRIDGEPORT. Pitcher Walter "the Big Train" Johnson was a speedball marvel. In October 1912, the righty visited the Remington Arms Company on Barnum Avenue, where F.C. Lane of *Baseball Magazine* had arranged to have Johnson's pitches clocked at the factory's bullet-testing laboratory. Throwing into a specially designed wooden framework while wearing street clothes, the Big Train was still clocked at 83 miles per hour. (Photograph courtesy of National Baseball Hall of Fame Library, Cooperstown, New York.)

PROPELLED TO VICTORY. The 1936 Industrial League champion Sikorsky Aviators pose in front of a Sikorsky S-42 Trans-Oceanic Flying Clipper outside the Lordship plant. Going into the final game of the season, the Aviators and the General Electric team were tied with 11-2 records. In a precursor to the pennant-deciding game, the teams faced each other in an employees Tuberculosis Relief Association fund-raiser. Interest in these teams was so intense that 5,000 fans turned out for the charity game. The Sikorsky Aviators would win the Industrial League championship the following week with a 9-1 victory over the General Electric team. Pictured, from left to right, are the following: (front row) A. Hovan, P. Baker, F. Marino, W. Scholz, and E. McQuillan; (back row) F. Bettiger, R. Oktayec, M. Buckmir, J. Dargenio, J. Klevecz, captain F. Parez, manager C. Naldandian, and president K. Leaman. (Photograph courtesy of Mickey Buckmir.)

CRANE VALVE NO. 2 IS NO. 1. Industrial League team Crane Valve Company No. 2 finished the 1909 season just one game ahead of their rivals, Crane No. 1. The team is pictured with four trophies. The Kinder Cup (right) was awarded to first baseman Walter "Shorty" Elwood (middle row, fourth from left) for highest batting average among Industrial League infielders. The Elmendorf Cup (left) was presented to the winner of the three-game series between the two Crane Valve teams. (Photograph courtesy of Historical Collections, Bridgeport Public Library.)

UNDERWOOD ELLIOTT-FISHER. The Underwood portable typewriter was such a hit in 1920 that the main plant in Hartford needed to expand. Bridgeport's Underwood Typewriter plant No. 2 was located on Broad Street in the old Bullard Machine Shop. When Sunstrand Adding Machine of Rockford, Illinois, and the Elliott-Fisher Company of Harrisburg, Pennsylvania, merged and moved to Bridgeport in 1933, they formed Underwood Elliott-Fisher. Before being razed in 1999, the abandoned factory was located across the street from the Ballpark at Harbor Yard. (Photograph courtesy of the Bridgeport Bluefish.)

NEW TEAM, NEW CHAMPIONS. In the early 1930s, the Kline family relocated with the Elliott-Fisher Company, from Harrisburg, Pennsylvania, to Bridgeport. John (center field), his brother Harry (second base), and Harry Kline Jr. (mascot) were all part of Underwood Elliott-Fisher's first Industrial League team in 1934. Underwood clinched the championship that summer with an 8-2 record. Shown here are Harry Kline Jr. (front row, third from left) and John Kline and Harry Kline Sr. (middle row, fourth and fifth from left). (Photograph courtesy of Fred and Violet [Kline] Biebel.)

THE FRISBIE PIE TEAM, THE 1930S. The Frisbie Pie Company, located on Kossuth Street, was well known for its tasty desserts. Legend has it that workers tossing Frisbie pie tins back and forth during breaks became the inspiration for the better-known Wham-O plastic disc. Perhaps the workers were practicing their sidearm deliveries. Frisbie Pie fielded a baseball team in the 1936 Morning Glory League along with clubs in Bridgeport's Industrial Softball League during the Great Depression. (Photograph courtesy of Anne Brignolo and Historical Collections, Bridgeport Public Library.)

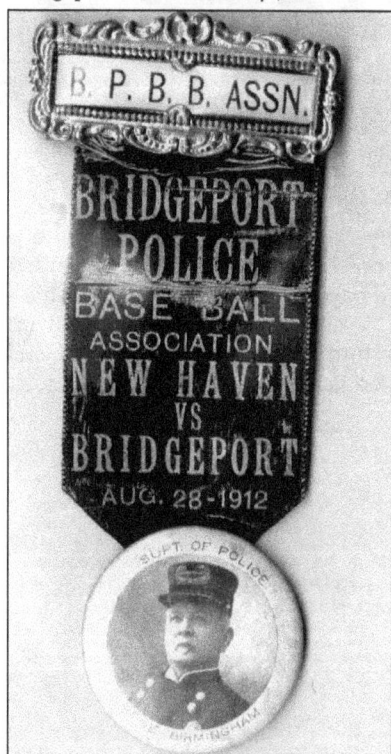

STEALING BASES, BRIDGEPORT'S POLICE TEAMS. Bridgeport's finest have fielded teams since the 19th century. In 1909, Bridgeport's men in blue participated in a statewide Police League, and charity games for the Police Sick Benefit Fund were a common event. This badge is from an August 28, 1912 fund-raiser when the Bridgeport team played their New Haven counterparts at Newfield Park. The Bridgeport Police team took the 1912 series against New Haven two games to none.

THE 1916 ROSEBUDS, SENIOR CITY LEAGUE. Bridgeport's Senior City League had featured outstanding baseball since the late 19th century. One of the league's longest-running teams was the Rosebuds. At the time, team headquarters were located on Berkshire Avenue. The 1916 Senior League championship club includes, from left to right, the following: (front row) Stephen Halapin, Ray Schorndorf, John Gabor, and John Creevy; (middle row) Frank Kohout, Andy Bobalki, John Sank, and John Shea; (back row) Michael Arnolsky (manager), Michael A. Sterback, Al Bakos, John Pjura, and Sam Kockiss. (Photograph courtesy of Historical Collections, Bridgeport Public Library.)

MR. MACK RETURNS. In September 1940, Connie Mack and his Philadelphia Athletics arrived early for an exhibition game at Schwarz Field, against promoter Carl Brunetto's squad. Learning the city's plans for a welcoming parade, Mr. Mack raced back to the train station to take his place in the march. Here, the venerable Hall of Fame manager (right) is pictured outside the Rosebud Athletic Association on Barnum Avenue with member Michael Sterback, one of the exhibition game organizers. (Photograph courtesy of Historical Collections, Bridgeport Public Library.)

THE SENIOR CITY LEAGUE WHITE EAGLES, 1927. The Polish National Alliance White Eagles team won the Senior City League championship in 1927. A Bridgeport baseball tradition pitted the winners of the Senior and Junior Leagues in a city title match at season's end. The year 1927 marked the first time two teams from the same order faced each other. Down by six runs in the fifth inning of the big game, the White Eagle Seniors roared back and defeated ace southpaw Johnny Michaels 13-7. (Photograph courtesy of Greater Bridgeport Oldtimer's Athletic Association.)

LEN "BO" BENEDETTO SR. The diamond accomplishments of Len Benedetto Sr. are well known. Throughout the 1930s, he was an outstanding batter and first baseman for the Senior League Iroquois, White Eagles, and Rosebuds, and he played for the Industrial League Singer company squad. Singer first baseman Benedetto is pictured stretching from the bag to make the out. (Photograph courtesy of Len "Butch" Benedetto.)

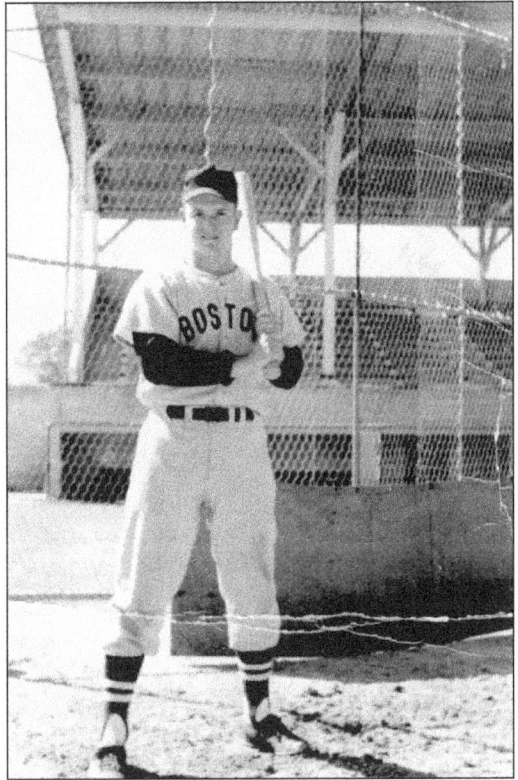

"BUTCH" BENEDETTO, SON OF "BO." Outfielder Len "Butch" Benedetto played four years of professional ball in the Red Sox organization. His best year came in 1961 with the Olean, New York Red Sox. In 418 at bats, Len hit 17 home runs with 93 RBIs and batted .321. Len's average was fourth best in the New York–Penn League. The batting title went to Atanasio Perez, better known as Tony of the Cincinnati Reds. (Photograph courtesy of Len "Butch" Benedetto.)

BUTCH AND YAZ. "Butch" Benedetto began his baseball career on William Ham Field in Bridgeport's South End. He played on the 1957 New England Champion Bridgeport Highlanders team of the Senior City League. In November 1958, he was signed by the Red Sox for a $20,000 bonus and was assigned to Ocala. From February through March 1959, his roommate was future Red Sox great Carl Yastrzemski. About 10 years later, roommates Yaz (left) and Butch Benedetto were reunited in Fort Lauderdale. (Photograph courtesy of Len "Butch" Benedetto.)

BRIDGEPORT'S SENIOR CITY LEAGUE GLORY CONTINUES. The year 1996 marked the ninth of 12 consecutive Senior City League championships for Stratford Ale House. That summer, the powerhouse team traveled to Louisville, Kentucky, and won the National Amateur Baseball Federation title. These team members are, from left to right, as follows: (front row) Maurice Scioletti, Matt Van Etten, John Figmic, Jeff Rotteck, and Albert Carrara; (middle row) Kevin Williams (coach), Mike Bennett, Paul Caseria, Jay McDougall, Rich Licursi, Kevin Kerkes, and John DelVecchio; (back row) John Breiner (sponsor), Jim Sarantides, Dave Lanese, Scott Szturma, Jim Tonelli, Tom Saxa, Jon Goode, Juan Lopez, Mick Buckmir, and Mickey Buckmir (manager). John Cocca, Jerry LaPenta, and Brian Muthersbaugh were not present when this picture was taken. (Photograph courtesy of Mickey Buckmir.)

THE CATHOLIC SOKOLS, 1927–1928. The day after Lindbergh returned to America from his historic solo flight across the Atlantic, Bridgeport's Catholic Sokols began their own triumphant journey. On June 12, 1927, the Catholic Sokols (Slovak for "falcon") played and won their inaugural game. The team continued to win. They completed the 1927 Connecticut Catholic Sokol League schedule undefeated, winning three independent games, and were victorious over their western counterparts from Pennsylvania. When the infield dust settled, they were 16-0. (Photograph courtesy of Historical Collections, Bridgeport Public Library.)

CHURCH LEAGUES. Bridgeport baseball was pervasive. Every major social and work-related organization fielded a team. Churches were represented in both the Senior and Junior Holy Name Baseball Leagues. This photograph of the St. Cyrils team, Senior Holy Name Champs, dates from the late 1940s. It was taken on the front steps of Saints Cyril and Methodius on Church Street. (Photograph courtesy of Mickey Buckmir.)

101

THE MERCANTILE LEAGUE. Howland's Department Store was one of several retailers to have their own team. They played against other stores, such as D.M. Read, American Hardware Stores, and Bridgeport Public Market, in the city's Mercantile League. Howland's celebrated the national pastime and attracted customers by distributing copies of *Official Base Ball Rules* in 1922. (Booklet courtesy of Bruce Williams.)

OFFICIAL

BASE BALL RULES

ADOPTED BY

AMERICAN AND NATIONAL LEAGUES

AND THE

NATIONAL ASSOCIATION OF

PROFESSIONAL BASE BALL LEAGUES

OFFICIAL PUBLICATION

1922

Distributed by

HOWLAND'S

BRIDGEPORT,   CONN.

HOWLAND'S. Bridgeport's popular department store was located on the corner of Main and Cannon Streets (the current site of the Fairfield County Courthouse). In the 1920s, customers found sporting goods on the fourth floor, along with Victrolas. (Photograph courtesy of Historical Collections, Bridgeport Public Library.)

Eight

BRIDGEPORT'S BOYS OF SUMMER

MAUVE DECADE TIGERS. This photograph, most likely taken in the 1890s, features the Bridgeport Tigers. The team played their games in the North End. From left to right are the following: (front row) Jack Haggerty and Charley McCullough; (middle row) Bob Egan, Jim McCullough, manager Eddie Menard, Patsy Cunningham, and Fay; (back row) Skinny Kelly, Cap Seeley, and Dave Poland. (Photograph courtesy of Historical Collections, Bridgeport Public Library.)

JOHNNY MICHAELS, 1927. Local hero Johnny Michaels (second row, sixth from left) pitched for Harding High School and later for the 1928–1930 Bears. The Bears southpaw posted a 16-7 record his last season with Bridgeport. Fans that summer recall the crowds that turned out whenever Michaels pitched against Hartford. (*The Stylus* photograph courtesy of Ben Murphy.)

JOHNNY MICHAELS'S DAUGHTER DIANE SHARES A FAMILY STORY. Boston Red Sox pitcher John Michaels's sole major-league win came against the Yankees in the nightcap of a July 2, 1932 double header. The Sox won 6-5, and Michaels held the Babe and Gehrig hitless. Michaels faced Ruth again later that year. "With the Sox losing badly," daughter Diane explained, "the catcher kept signaling my dad for the fast ball and my father kept shaking him off. The delay caused the manager to come out to the mound and he told my father, 'We're not in it, so give the fans what they came out to see. Throw Ruth the fast ball.' That home run Ruth hit was the farthest my father ever saw." (Photograph courtesy of Kitty and John Midney.)

THE 1928 WARREN HARDING HIGH SCHOOL BASEBALL TEAM. The school's outstanding pitcher was Sam Dizenzo. On June 2, the righty threw a no-hitter against Ansonia while fanning 11. Six days later, facing Derby, he struck out 13 and allowed only two hits in Harding's 6-1 victory. The Presidents took the city championship on June 16 while Dizenzo mowed down 16 Central High batters. The Harding team includes, from left to right, the following: (front row) J. Jacobs, R. Supersano, E. Swezey, R. Kane, W. Lukachik, and W. Carroll; (back row) coach Mead, W. Cholko, J. Pivarnick, W. Schrieber, S. Miska, S. Dizenzo, and manager Murphy. (Photograph courtesy of Ben Murphy.)

MANAGER MURPHY. Seventy-five years after Ben Murphy managed the 1928 Harding baseball team, he recalls the season with pride. As manager, Ben received a team letter. Murphy smiles, "I'll never forget sewing that gold H on my sweater as long as I live!" The best Bridgeport pitcher he ever saw was Harding's Sam Dizenzo. (Photograph courtesy of Ben Murphy.)

THE UNIVERSITY SCHOOL TEAM, 1927. Founded in 1892, the University School's sports program was active from the 1890s through the 1940s. Their baseball team played games against other schools and social clubs. The private school team of 1927 is pictured at Seaside Park. Mark Richardson, the school's owner, is standing on the far right. (Photograph courtesy of Historical Collections, Bridgeport Public Library.)

A BALLPARK IS BORN. Playing fields were a precious commodity in Bridgeport. In the summer of 1948, 15-year-old Charlie Rich and friends searched for a convenient open location to play ball. The site they found was on an old landfill on the corner of Carroll Avenue and Orange Street near the Bridgeport-Stratford town line. The boys worked hard for weeks cleaning the field of debris. The Buckley Brothers fuel tanks along Johnsons Creek are seen beyond center field, and the tiny Lordship Road bridge is barely visible on the left. Charlie convinced a helpful city worker to grade the area, and the diamond became playable. (Photograph courtesy of Charlie Rich.)

106

NEW TEAM, NEW DUGOUT. Manager Charlie Rich originally thought about calling his team the Warriors, but after reading about Jackie Robinson's heroics with Brooklyn's Triple A affiliate, the Montreal Royals, Rich named his team the Royals. This photograph, taken on July 15, 1949, features, from left to right, Dominick Sportelli, Raymond Brockett, Charlie Rich, Alex Patuzzi, Fred Voccola, Ray Bredice, John Farrell, Jack Hulford, and George Bush. Orange Street is just behind the dugout. (Photograph courtesy of Charlie Rich.)

REMEMBERING THE IRON HORSE. The Royals loved Lou Gehrig and his determined, gentlemanly approach to baseball and life. In 1949, they decided to celebrate the Yankees first baseman's memory by naming their new grounds Lou Gehrig Memorial Field. Pictured alongside the team's hand-painted sign are, from left to right, Charlie Rich, Al Patuzzi, Jack Hulford, Raymond Brockett, Walter White, John Farrell, Dick White, and Dominick Sportelli (standing). (Photograph courtesy of Charlie Rich scrapbooks.)

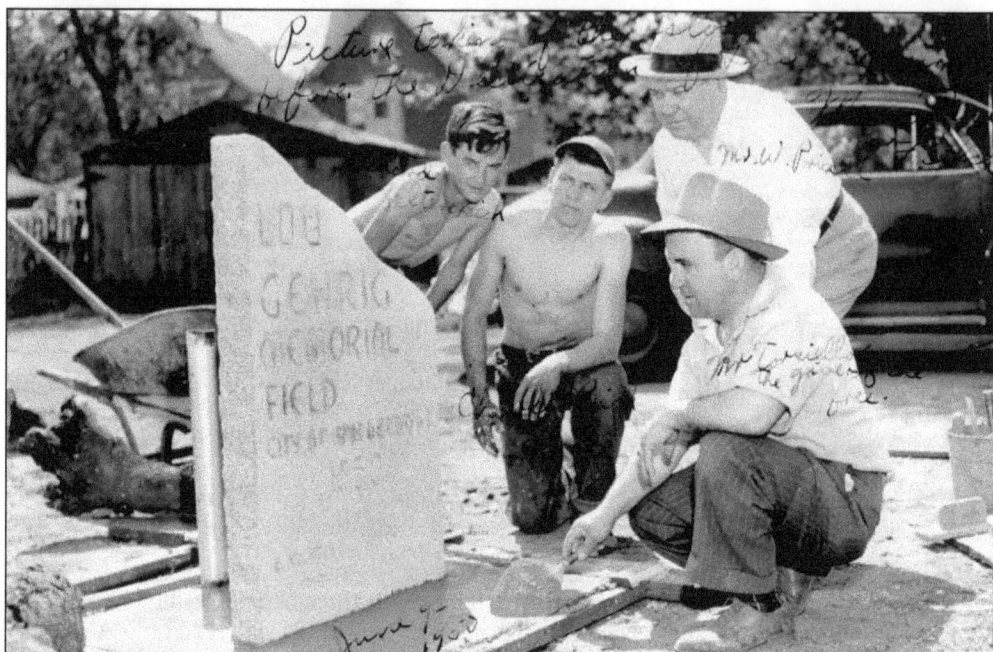

THE TEAM IS DISCOVERED. Ethel Beckwith, a reporter with the *Sunday Herald*, noticed the Royals at play and fell in love with the boys' dedication that transformed a dump into a diamond. A series of articles in the *Herald* sparked generosity from area businesses. Honeyspot Monument Works owner Nicholas Torsiello donated a granite monument to commemorate the grounds. The Lou Gehrig Memorial Field stone was placed along the first base line in early June 1950. In this view, Richard Seltenrich (Royals player), Charlie Rich (manager), and Billy Prince (former state athletic commissioner and president of the Herald Sportsmen's Club) assist Torsiello in setting the stone. (Photograph courtesy of Charlie Rich.)

ROYAL MASCOT. During an afternoon practice, a stray cat joined the team in the dugout. Taking a page from H. Allen Smith's 1946 book *Rhubarb*, the team named their newest fan after the novel's feline protagonist. Rhubarb moved in with the Rich family and attended every Royals game. (Photograph courtesy of Charlie Rich.)

MOM GEHRIG. At the time, Lou Gehrig's mother Christine lived in the nearby community of Devon, Connecticut. She was overwhelmed when she heard the news of the Bridgeport boys cherishing the name of her son. At the invitation of the *Bridgeport Herald*, Christine Gehrig participated in the field's dedication ceremony. Here, she is shown proudly displaying a photograph of Lou. (Photograph from the *Bridgeport Herald*, May 28, 1950, Charlie Rich scrapbooks.)

THE OFFICIAL DEDICATION. On Tuesday, July 13, 1950, some 15,000 residents lined the streets of Bridgeport's East End to view the parade celebrating the Royals and their ballpark. The procession was a special feature of the second annual Barnum Festival and culminated in the official dedication of Lou Gehrig Memorial Field. Pictured here riding at the head of the parade are, from left to right, Mayor Jasper McLevy and guest of honor Christine Gehrig, mother of the Yankees great. (Photograph courtesy of Charlie Rich.)

THE PARADE ROUTE. Members of the Royals rode in two National Guard jeeps while school marching bands played "Take Me Out to the Ball Game." Following the boys were the Bridgeport Bees, Barnum Festival royalty, Billy Prince president of the Herald Sportsmen's Club, and New York Yankees secretary Jack Farrell. The parade began at 5:00 p.m. on the Old Mill Green, proceeded down East Main Street to Stratford Avenue, and finished at the Royals ballpark at Carroll Avenue and Orange Street. (Photograph courtesy of Charlie Rich.)

THE MONUMENT UNVEILING. More than 4,000 people gathered for the field's dedication ceremony. Mayor McLevy and Yankees secretary Farrell provided remarks. Among those on hand are, from left to right, Billy Prince, Stan Buckmir (in Royals jacket), and Ethel Beckwih (in hat). Charlie Rich is raising the flag over the monument inscribed with "Lou Gehrig Memorial Field . . . City of Bridgeport 1950 . . . A Great Ball Player . . . The Iron Man of Baseball." It was reported that Christine Gehrig cried when she removed the cloth from the stone. (Photograph courtesy of Charlie Rich.)

A Moment in the Sun. Following the monument's unveiling, the Colonial League Bridgeport Bees played the Royals in a three-inning exhibition game. Over half a century later, Royals manager Charlie Rich smiles how his team was allowed to defeat the Bees 2-0. This double-exposure hauntingly portrays Charlie Rich on the mound delivering a pitch to the Bees, a line of spectators crowding the baseline while, ever so faintly, Mom Gehrig proudly watches the game. (Photograph courtesy of Charlie Rich.)

The Day Gehrig Died, Again. In the autumn of 1955, Charlie Rich returned to Bridgeport from military duty to discover his beloved ball field had gone fallow. Charlie went to work raking bottles and rubbish strewn around the abandoned diamond when a neighbor informed him that the field lay in the path of the proposed Interstate 95 thruway. Charlie put the rake away, and within weeks, earthmovers decimated the grounds. In a few months, pylons and concrete distorted the landscape. The monument commemorating Lou Gehrig Memorial Field was removed for safekeeping with the hope of a future dedication at a new site. Over time, the monument has been lost and has yet to be recovered. (Photograph courtesy of Charlie Rich.)

HAPPY BEES, CANDLELITE STADIUM, 1949. Shown here are, from left to right, outfielder Joe Biros, official Bees batboy Gerald McDougall, ball boy Vinny Noce, and first baseman Jim Paules. McDougall won his summer job after being selected from 650 entries in a contest sponsored by the *Bridgeport Herald*. Twelve-year-old Noce already worked in the clubhouse. As ball boy, he was responsible for refreshing the home plate ump's supply of baseballs, catching balls rolling off the backstop screen, retrieving foul balls, and rubbing the gloss off new baseballs as well as bagging peanuts for vendors. (Photograph courtesy of Jim Paules.)

BRIDGEPORT APPEARS IN THE 1950 LITTLE LEAGUE WORLD SERIES. In 1949, the Bridgeport Original Little League made it to the Nationals in Williamsport, Pennsylvania, but were eliminated in the second round. The team repeated their Connecticut State Championship in 1950 and advanced all the way to the Little League World Series. Connecticut's 1950 champs are, from left to right, as follows: (front row) coach Don Iodice, Mickey Buchmir, Charlie Casano, Richard Burlant, bat boy John Fox Jr., Jim Lesko, Frank Saccone, Lou Viglione, and manager John Panula; (back row) Dennis Russell, Ron Ulbrick, Bob Kuraska, Ron Liptak, John Lewis, Ken Samu, Tom Norko, and Bobby Paulin. (Photograph courtesy of Mickey Buckmir.)

GAME ONE OF THE 1950 LITTLE LEAGUE NATIONALS. On the afternoon of August 24, 1950, Bridgeport third baseman Ken Samu slid safely under the Clinton, South Carolina catcher with the winning run. Samu scored on Lou Viglione's seventh-inning squeeze bunt. This was extra-inning play since regulation Little League games last six frames. Bridgeport pitcher John Lewis allowed only four hits while striking out 14 players. The 3-2 victory over South Carolina advanced Bridgeport to the semifinals. (Photograph courtesy of Historical Collections, Bridgeport Public Library.)

THE GAME TWO SCARE, AUGUST 25, 1950. Bridgeport second baseman Mickey Buckmir was struck in the left temple and cheek with a pitch thrown by Maryland's Roy Stotler in the top of the sixth. Helmets were not used then, and Buckmir's only protection was his cap. Immediately after Buckmir was hit, coach Iodice and manager Panula comforted the player. Maryland catcher Ken Dudley made sure Mickey was okay, and Rich Burlant came down from the first base coaching box to check on his teammate. Charlie Casano went in as a courtesy runner, but Buckmir went back to the keystone bag in the bottom of the inning. In the end, Bridgeport beat Maryland with a score of 6-2. (Photograph courtesy of Mickey Buckmir.)

A CLOSE GAME AND AN ERROR. Before the deciding August 26, 1950 Little League World Series match, the Bridgeport team was presented during pregame ceremonies in Williamsport, Pennsylvania. In the final game, Bridgeport was defeated by Texas 2-1. Little League officials did not pay close attention when creating Bridgeport's sign. Connecticut is misspelled. (Photograph courtesy of Mickey Buckmir.)

114

FORD FRICK COMES TO BRIDGEPORT. On September 2, 1951, the Bridgeport Howland's-sponsored team captured the National Junior League championship (for boys 13 to 15 years old) by defeating Middletown 9-3. Tournament games were played at Seaside Village Field in the South End. Ford Frick, president of the National League, came to Bridgeport by train to attend the deciding game. In this view, the man in front is unidentified. In the back are Ford Frick (left) and William Ham. (Photograph courtesy of Historical Collections, Bridgeport Public Library.)

FRICK AND HAM, SEPTEMBER 2, 1951. A noon reception for the competing National Junior League teams was held at the University of Bridgeport's Marina Hall the day of the final game. From left to right are John Fox Jr., Howland's bat boy; Ford Frick, National League president; Howland's Department Store players Ron Liptak and Ken Samu (too old to play with Little League); and William Ham. (Photograph courtesy of Historical Collections, Bridgeport Public Library.)

HAM, FRICK, AND MOM GEHRIG AT NATIONAL JUNIOR LEAGUE RECEPTION. Bridgeport sports enthusiast William Ham loved baseball and helping children. He donated land to create the ballpark at Seaside Village. Ford Frick was president of the National League from 1935 to 1951 and helped create the Baseball Hall of Fame. He later threatened to suspend any team that boycotted games played by Jackie Robinson. He was named commissioner of baseball in 1951. Lou Gehrig's mother lived in Devon, Connecticut, and loved to support area baseball. Shown here from left to right are Ham, Frick, and Mom Gehrig. (Photograph courtesy of Historical Collections, Bridgeport Public Library.)

ACCUSTOMED TO THE SALTY BREEZE. With Long Island Sound in the background, Bassick High School plays Fairfield Prep at Seaside Park's Diamond No. 1 in the spring of 1972. The lefty delivering the pitch is Bassick's Phil Nastu. Soon, he would confront the stiff winds of Candlestick Park as a member of the San Francisco Giants. In the ready stance is second baseman George Saccone, who batted a whopping .524 that season. (Photograph courtesy of Phil Nastu.)

116

DREAMS COME TRUE AT ZOLIE'S PIZZA. This is a 1968 photograph of the Bridgeport Original Pony League team sponsored by Zolie's Pizza House. Dreams of going to the majors came true for one boy in this picture. Phil Nastu pitched for the San Francisco Giants from 1978 to 1980. From left to right are the following: (front row) Billy Roman, Mike Kuric, Robby Kasparek, Mark Windsor, Mike Kerwin, Bob Speer, and Al LeClaire; (back row) Tom Cipu, Bob Charity, Nastu, Ken Petrella, Brian Kelps, Tom Lula, Jim Dinunzo, and coach-sportswriter Ray Van Stone. (Photograph courtesy of Phil Nastu.)

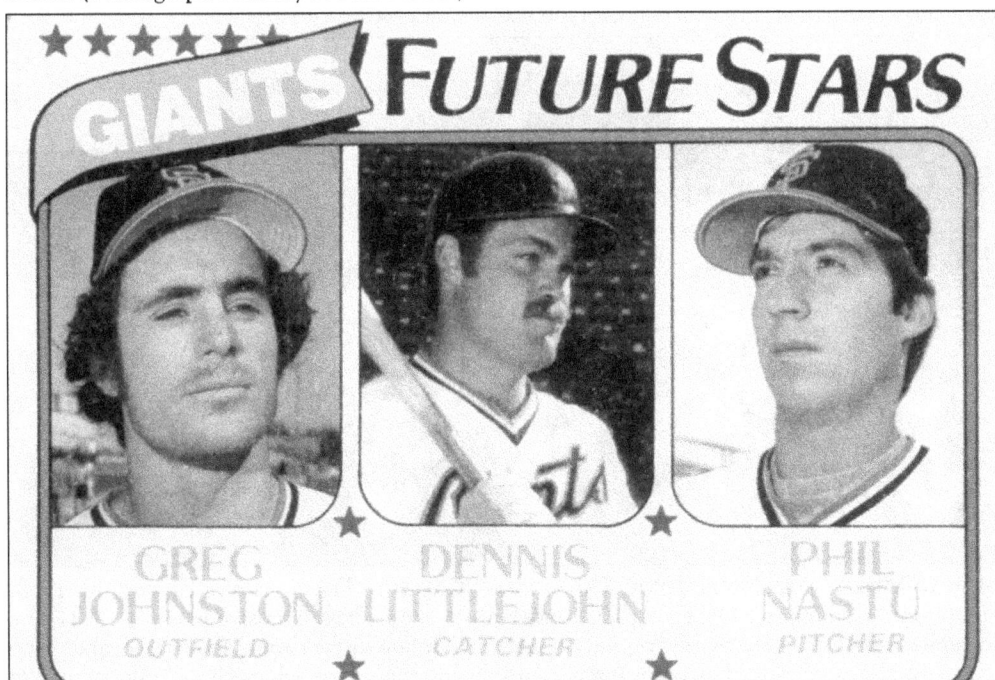

PHIL NASTU'S TOPPS BASEBALL CARD, 1980. Known for his roundhouse curve, Bridgeport athlete Phil Nastu played in the Giants organization for four years. He appeared in a total of 34 games with San Francisco from 1978 to 1980. (Courtesy of Topps Company.)

117

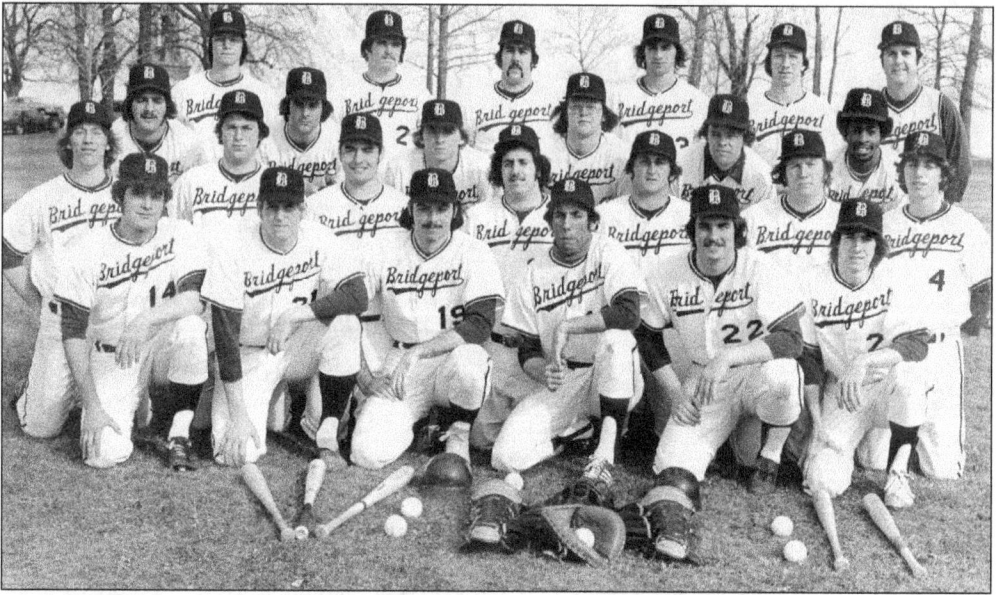

TALENT RICH UNIVERSITY OF BRIDGEPORT, 1974. San Francisco Giants pitcher Phil Nastu (front row, far right) grew up in Bridgeport's West End. He was an outstanding player with the University of Bridgeport. One season, he posted a .69 ERA with the Purple Knights. His senior year (1976), Phil played center field when not pitching and won the team's batting title. Teammate Nick Giaquinto (second row, far left) went on to play four years in the NFL. The running back appeared in Super Bowls XVII and XVIII. Giaquinto became head baseball coach of Sacred Heart University, Fairfield, Connecticut, in 1988. (Photograph courtesy of Phil Nastu.)

MERCY, MERCY THE HOUSATONIC COMMUNITY COLLEGE TEAM, 1981. Started in 1969, Housatonic Community College (HCC) baseball fielded its best offensive team in 1981. The squad set a school record by hitting nine home runs in one district tournament ballgame. The Mercy Rule was employed by umps many times during the season when HCC built incredible leads. The 1981 team finished ninth in the NJCAA World Series. Including postseason games, HCC achieved a record of 38-13. Budget deficits later caused the school to eliminate its sports program in 1997. (Photograph courtesy of Housatonic Community College.)

Nine

FROM BEARS TO BEES
TO BLUEFISH

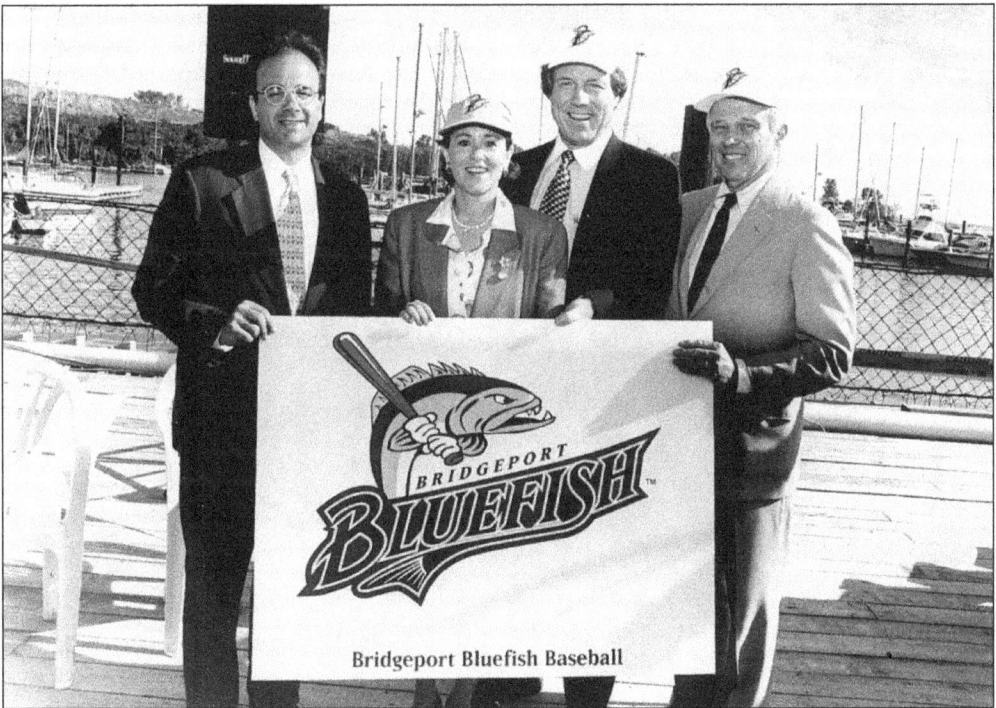

BASEBALL RETURNS. The owners of the yet unnamed Atlantic League Bridgeport baseball club held a press conference at Captain's Cove on May 29, 1997. A crowd had gathered on the dock overlooking Black Rock Harbor that sparkling day to witness the unveiling of the team's name. Shown here are, from left to right, Bridgeport Mayor Joseph Ganim, along with team principle owners and co-founders Mary-Jane Foster, Mickey Herbert, and Jack McGregor proudly displaying the Bluefish logo. (Photograph courtesy of the Bridgeport Bluefish.)

UNDER THE INFIELD. The Ballpark at Harbor Yard opened a new chapter in Bridgeport's history. Nestled between the tracks of the Metro-North railroad and elevated Interstate 95 thruway, the ballfield breathes new life into an abandoned industrial area. The ballpark rests on the site of the Sprague Meter Company and the Jenkins Brothers Valves Company (pictured here). The Jenkins complex was originally the Eaton, Cole, and Burnham Company (1876) and was later purchased by Crane Valve in 1904. The factory became Jenkins Valves from 1920 through 1988. (Photograph courtesy of Historical Collections, Bridgeport Public Library.)

A CENTURY'S WORTH OF BRICK. To make way for the new ballpark, the demolition of the sprawling Jenkins Valves factory began in late May 1997. (Photograph courtesy of Frank W. Decerbo Jr.)

120

HARBOR YARD CONSTRUCTION, 1997–1998. The ballpark is named in celebration of neighboring Bridgeport Harbor and the adjacent railroad that spurred the city's industrial growth. It took less than a year to raze the buildings on the site and build the ballpark. The Kasper Group of Bridgeport coordinated the stadium project. The construction manager was C.R. Klewin Construction. Design Exchange of Newark, Delaware, designed the ballpark. The stadium provides a feeling of community. Ferries of the Bridgeport and Port Jefferson Steamboat Company are visible from the stadium, and passing trains toot their whistles to waving fans. (Photograph courtesy of Morgan Kaolian/AEROPIX.)

THE SPORTS COMPLEX IN DOWNTOWN BRIDGEPORT, 2003. The Ballpark at Harbor Yard is located on the corner of Broad Street and South Frontage Road with a seating capacity of 5,300 plus another 200 for standing room. Outfield dimensions are 325 feet (left field), 400 feet (center field), and 325 feet (right field). The Arena at Harbor Yard, home of the American Hockey League's Bridgeport Sound Tigers, is just beyond left field. (Photograph courtesy of Morgan Kaolian/AEROPIX.)

121

A SOUVENIR CARD. The Ballpark at Harbor Yard was the home field to two Atlantic League teams in 1998—the Bluefish and the Newark Bears. The latter club called Bridgeport home that single season while their stadium was constructed.

OPENING DAY TICKETS. Opening day came on May 21, 1998. Bridgeport defeated the Newark Bears 8-4 in front of a sold-out standing room crowd of 5,500.

EAGER FOR A LOOK AT THE NEW BALL YARD. A crowd gathers outside the Ballpark at Harbor Yard on May 21, 1998, waiting for opening day festivities. A sellout crowd of 5,500 fans was on hand to help usher in a new era of Bridgeport baseball. (Photograph courtesy of the Bridgeport Bluefish.)

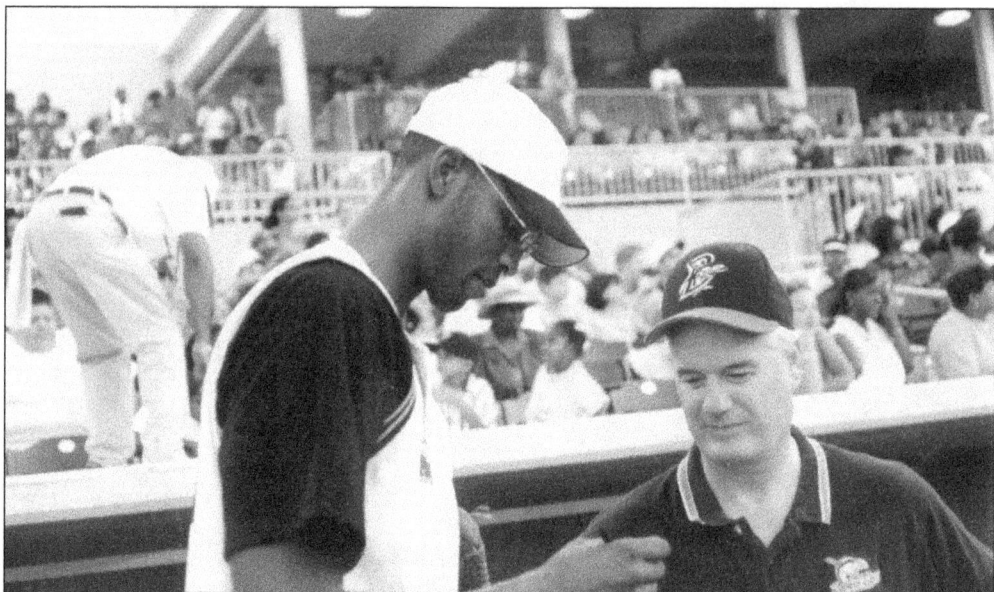

KEN PAUL, PRESENT AT THE CREATION. Ken Paul was in charge of putting Bridgeport's Atlantic League team together. He was responsible for start-up activities, including the name-the-team contest and recruiting front office staff. He is a senior vice president and co-owner. Ken (right) is pictured here at Harbor Yard with New York Knicks star Charles Smith during a Charles Smith Foundation charity softball game. (Photograph courtesy of Ken Paul.)

MEET THE PLAYERS. Members of a professional Bridgeport team are announced in front of a home crowd for the first time in 48 years. The Bluefish are standing along the first base foul line near their dugout. The first four Bluefish are, from left to right, manager Willie Upshaw, bench coach Mel Wearing Jr., Duane Singleton (No. 25), and Mike Felder. (Photograph courtesy of the Bridgeport Bluefish.)

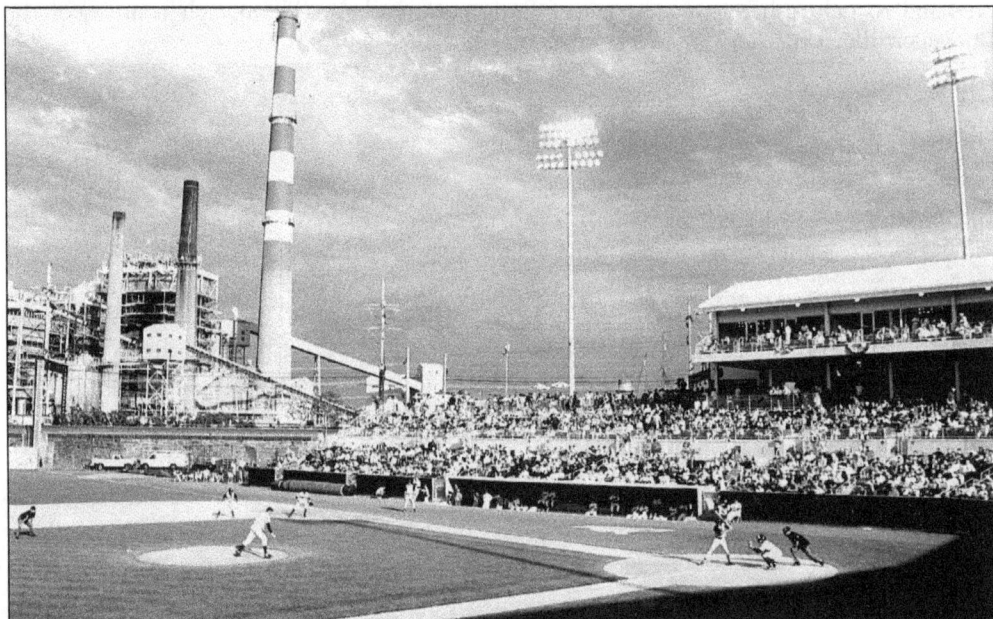

A BEAUTIFUL DAY TO START A LEAGUE. This photograph taken on opening day, May 21, 1998, from the Harbor Yard left-field stands captures Al Sontag firing the ball to catcher Terry McGriff. Smokestacks of the former United Illuminating facility loom beyond the right-field bleachers. The tallest of the three stacks can be seen as far away as Long Island. The stack is a Bridgeport landmark, and talk of painting it in the likeness of a baseball bat has circulated since Harbor Yard opened. (Photograph courtesy of Robert L. Harrison.)

THE INAUGURAL BLUEFISH TEAM. The 1998 Atlantic League Bridgeport Bluefish won the first half title, thereby clinching a spot in the Championship Series. The Atlantic City Surf took the postseason crown by winning the best-of-five series three games to one. The overall 64-36 record for the 1998 Bluefish was tops in the league. First baseman Kinnis Pledger was named co-MVP, Willie Upshaw was named Manager of the Year, and Charlie Dowd was honored as Executive of the Year. The members of the 1998 Bluefish are, from left to right, as follows: (front row) unidentified clubhouse personnel, Brian Cornelius, Kennis Pledger, Mel Wearing Jr. (player-coach), Willie Upshaw (manager), David Osteen (pitching coach), Mark Lambert (coach), Jim Klemyk, and unidentified clubhouse personnel; (middle row) Joe Walker, Lamont Edwards, Terry McGriff, Steve Renko, Adam Meinershagen, Al Sontag, Jason Yoder, Terry Rosenkranz, Carey Paige, Jose Cintron, and Gerald Davis; (back row) Duane Singleton, Mike Guilfoyle, Dan Fraraccio, Marshall Bennett, Mike Felder, James Landingham, Malcolm Cepeda, Asbel Ortiz, and Ruben Marquez. (Photograph courtesy of Brody Printing Company Inc.)

THE SQUID. Pitcher Al "the Squid" Sontag's delivery gave rise to his nickname. Opposing batters see a tangle of arms and legs unwinding as Al prepares to release the ball. Sontag owns the first victory in Bluefish history. He hurled for Bridgeport from 1998 to 2002 and served as pitching coach in 2001. In 2003, Al signed on as manager for the Macon Peaches in the Southeastern Professional Baseball League. (Photograph courtesy of Steve Raguskus.)

DURABLE MIKE GUILFOYLE. Guilfoyle is dedicated to the game he loves. In 1998 and in 2001, he led the Atlantic League in saves and represented Bridgeport in the Atlantic League's inaugural All-Star game. Starting his sixth season with the Bluefish in 2003, he is the only active player remaining from the original team. He is well known throughout Fairfield County for his work helping schoolchildren appreciate sports and education. (Photograph courtesy of the Bridgeport Bluefish.)

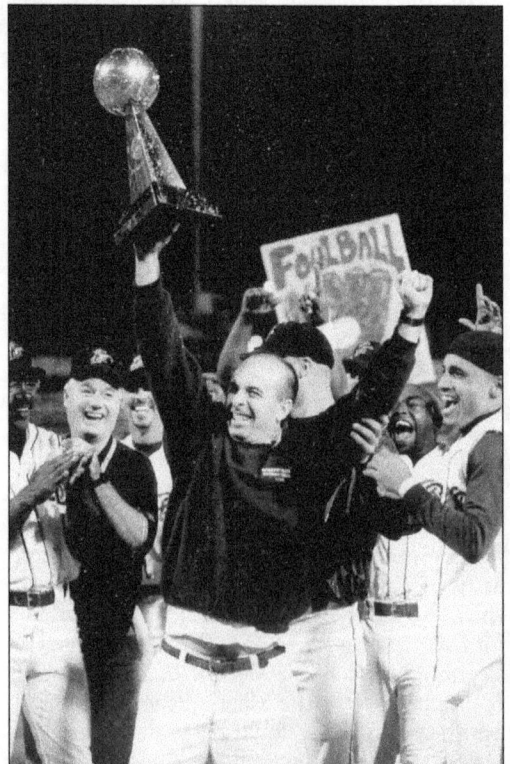

CHAMPIONSHIP ARCHITECT. Charlie Dowd was introduced as Bluefish general manager on the front steps of the team's original State Street offices on September 16, 1997. Just two years and three days later, he was on the infield of Harbor Yard lofting the Atlantic League Championship Trophy. (Photograph courtesy of the Connecticut Post and the Bridgeport Bluefish.)

THE BLUEFISH WIN THEIR FIRST ATLANTIC LEAGUE CHAMPIONSHIP, 1999. After pitcher Dave Adam secured the final out in Bridgeport's three-game sweep of the Somerset Patriots, this pile-on of celebrating ballplayers occurred. Gathering themselves, the Bluefish led a spontaneous conga line in cleats along Harbor Yard's loge walkway and back onto the field again. (Photograph courtesy of the Bridgeport Bluefish.)

BRIDGEPORT BLUEFISH, 2002. The 2002 Bluefish won the North Division Titles in both the first and second halves of the season. They tied the league lead in victories in 2002 with a record of 71-55. The Bluefish are the winningest team in the five-year history of the Atlantic League, drawing just under one and a half million fans to Harbor Yard since the gates opened on May 21, 1998. (Photograph courtesy of the Bridgeport Bluefish.)

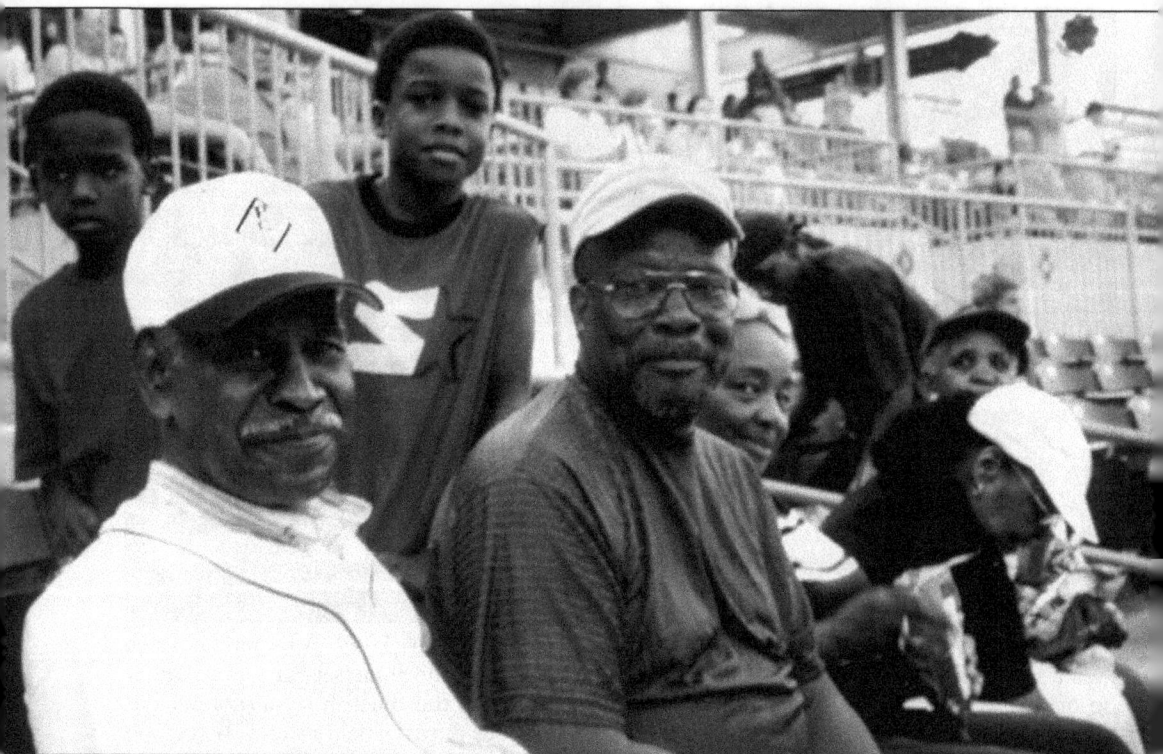

TURN BACK THE CLOCK. On August 14, 2002, the Bluefish celebrated the memory of the Park City Giants, one of Bridgeport's outstanding semiprofessional African American teams from the 1920s to the 1930s. During the game, the Bluefish wore replica jerseys from the 1925 Park City Giants. That evening Frank Bridgeforth, son of Park City Giants pitcher Edward Bridgeforth, toed the pitching rubber like his father did three quarters of a century ago, and threw out the ceremonial first pitch. Frank (foreground, far left) is seen here in the stands enjoying the game with his family.

Visit us at
arcadiapublishing.com

· ·

www.ingramcontent.com/pod-product-compliance
Lightning Source LLC
Chambersburg PA
CBHW080602110426
42813CB00006B/1384